PROFESSIONAL ANDROID WEARABLES

PROFESSIONAL

Android™ Wearables

David Cuartielles Ruiz
Andreas Göransson

wrox™
A Wiley Brand

Professional Android™ Wearables

Published by
John Wiley & Sons, Inc.
10475 Crosspoint Boulevard
Indianapolis, IN 46256
www.wiley.com

Copyright © 2015 by John Wiley & Sons, Inc., Indianapolis, Indiana

Published simultaneously in Canada

ISBN: 978-1-118-98685-1

ISBN: 978-1-118-98686-8 (ebk)

ISBN: 978-1-118-98687-5 (ebk)

Manufactured in the United States of America

10 9 8 7 6 5 4 3 2 1

For general information on our other products and services please contact our Customer Care Department within the United States at (877) 762-2974, outside the United States at (317) 572-3993 or fax (317) 572-4002.

Wiley publishes in a variety of print and electronic formats and by print-on-demand. Some material included with standard print versions of this book may not be included in e-books or in print-on-demand. If this book refers to media such as a CD or DVD that is not included in the version you purchased, you may download this material at http://booksupport.wiley.com. For more information about Wiley products, visit www.wiley.com.

Library of Congress Control Number: 2014948539

To Bobbie, my very patient 7-year-old daughter, for the time that writing this book took away from building robots with her.

—David Cuartielles Ruiz

To YOU, for reading this book. I hope you'll have fun with Android Wear!

—Andreas Göransson

ABOUT THE AUTHORS

DAVID CUARTIELLES is one of the founders of the Arduino platform. He also is a lecturer at Malmö University and other universities in Europe, where he teaches interaction designers and artists how to use technology as a tool in their creative process. David is very active in helping change how technology is taught at secondary schools and high schools around the world. He collaborates with several foundations (Intel, Telefonica, La Caixa, and AECID) to acquaint teachers with new technologies. His main research areas are the Internet of Things, wearables, and educational tools. He has coauthored a couple of books (two of them for Wrox), a series of dissemination articles for magazines on electronics, and several academic papers.

ANDREAS GÖRANSSON is a designer, author, teacher, researcher, and maker who works at Malmö University within many subjects and disciplines. Holding a BSc in interaction design, he strayed from that path a long time ago and got into the world of technology and programming. He is an open source advocate who loves to solve problems large and small. He has contributed to projects such as Arduino. He frequently attends conferences around the world as a listener and speaker. He enjoys exploring new airports.

ABOUT THE TECHNICAL EDITOR

 **ERIK HELLMAN** currently lives in Stockholm, Sweden, where he works as a Senior Android Engineer at Spotify. He has a long experience in the field of mobile development, starting with the early versions of Java ME and later working as the lead architect for Sony Ericsson and Sony Mobile on their Android projects. Due to his vast experience with Android, Erik is also part of the Google Developer Experts where he helps Google teach about their platform. Erik is the author of the book *Android Programming: Pushing the Limits* and can often be found speaking at various developer conferences across Europe. He spends his free time traveling with his wife, reading every sci-fi book he can get his hands on, and experimenting with electronics and food.

CREDITS

ACQUISITIONS EDITOR
Mariann Barsolo

PROJECT EDITOR
Christina Haviland

TECHNICAL EDITOR
Erik Hellman

PRODUCTION EDITOR
Dassi Zeidel

COPY EDITOR
Gayle Johnson

**MANAGER OF CONTENT DEVELOPMENT
AND ASSEMBLY**
Mary Beth Wakefield

MARKETING DIRECTOR
David Mayhew

MARKETING MANAGER
Carrie Sherrill

**PROFESSIONAL TECHNOLOGY & STRATEGY
DIRECTOR**
Barry Pruett

BUSINESS MANAGER
Amy Knies

ASSOCIATE PUBLISHER
Jim Minatel

PROJECT COORDINATOR, COVER
Patrick Redmond

PROOFREADER
Sarah Kaikini, Word One New York

INDEXER
John Sleeva

COVER DESIGNER
Wiley

COVER IMAGE
© iStock.com/dolgachov

ACKNOWLEDGMENTS

THIS BOOK wouldn't have been possible without my coauthor, Andreas, whom I have seen grow into an excellent programmer, capable of doing almost anything related to code. Thanks as well to Sergio Villalobos from LG's marketing department in Mexico, who gave us access to a real smartwatch while it was still impossible to get one in Sweden. To the unknown engineer at LG who kindly gave his watch to Sergio to give to us. To Troed Sångberg at Sony in Sweden who got us a Sony SmartWatch 3 to test the final chapters in the book. To Pontus Stalin at inUse for some other tools that also came in handy. To my whole team at Arduino Verkstad, who gave me emotional support just by being there—especially Mr. Duffy, who took some of the pictures for the book. Finally, to Laura, who made everything possible by helping in the day-to-day while I was writing.

—David Cuartielles Ruiz

THANKS FIRST TO MY COAUTHOR, friend, mentor, and former teacher for dragging me into this exciting world of tech! Who knows what I would have been doing today if I hadn't been introduced to The Lab at K3?

Also, a big thank you to the staff at Wiley for their support and vigilant efforts in producing this book. Thanks to Chris Haviland for her help and extreme patience with me and David since the beginning of this project. Also, I'd like to thank Bob Elliott for giving us the opportunity to work on one more book together; it's been an adventure, just like the first time. Erik Hellman and Jonas Bengtsson deserve a big thanks for helping us nail the technical side of the book.

A huge thank-you to Sergio Villalobos at LG for lending us a Wear device when none was available in Sweden. It definitely made this book much easier to write. Also, Troed Sångberg at Sony played a major part in finishing this book when he lent us a SmartWatch 3 to work on the newly released GPS libraries. Without these devices it would have been impossible to complete the book.

Finally, I'd like to extend my gratitude to friends and family for their patience during this time, and to Tony and Fernando for their support and fun conversations around all of our projects. Finally, I'd like to thank Katya for being an inspiration to me and for making me want to work twice as hard.

—Andreas Göransson

ACKNOWLEDGEMENTS

CONTENTS

INTRODUCTION

WEARABLES is an exciting field. It has existed commercially for more than a decade in the form of watches, headsets, clothes, activity trackers, and cameras. But only in the last few years have we seen devices so tiny and complex that we can truly call them wearable.

Google launched its Glass technology in 2012 with an impressive demo, showcasing not just how tiny the device is, but also all the functionality compressed into it. In 2014 Google continued on this path of wearable devices with its Android Wear SDK, which presents a new way of thinking about wearable devices. It is no longer a standalone device that can talk to your phone or computer; it is a device that *extends* your phone. This presents a unique new way of thinking about your personal devices. The phone is your primary device, and you can extend it with new functionality by connecting wearable devices to it.

Wearables is a field we've been researching for half a decade now, developing our own wearable devices that connect to personal devices for full functionality and connectivity. We've seen the possibilities in the field, and Android Wear can help us achieve them.

This book is a hands-on guide to wearables, with a focus on the Android Wear SDK. You will learn about the Android Wear SDK by building small sample programs—examples that can easily be implemented in larger applications. This book covers all the basic functionality of Android Wear.

WHO THIS BOOK IS FOR

This book is for anyone who wants to dive into wearables in general and Android Wear application development in particular. The information in this book covers the major parts of the new and exciting platform called Android Wear.

This book works well both as a reference for the experienced Android developer and as an introductory guide if you've recently started your adventures in Android. You should have at least some understanding of Android's basic components to fully grasp the content of this book.

If you've never worked with any kind of wearable device, you may enjoy Chapter 1, which introduces the topics of wearable research and history, and Chapter 2, which introduces the closely related field of the Internet of Things (IoT).

If you're an inexperienced Android developer eager to get started coding, Chapter 3 may be a good starting point for instructions on setting up your development environment and test-running your first Android Wear app.

If you're an experienced Android developer, you might want to start with Chapters 4 through 8 which discuss the new Android Wear APIs in detail.

Chapters 9, 10, and 11 exemplify Android Wear development in three simple projects that you can use as starting points for your own ideas. Before doing so, you should read Part II.

WHAT THIS BOOK COVERS

The book is divided into three parts, Part I offers basic theory about wearables and the related field of the Internet of Things in an easily digested way. Part II will give you a foundation in Googles Wearable platform, Android Wear, and Part III contains three easy-to-build projects.

Chapter 1 introduces the history of and research into wearables. Chapter 2 introduces the closely related field of the Internet of Things. Chapter 3 covers installing your development environment and preparing devices and emulators before you compile and run your first Android Wear application—Recipe Assistant.

Chapters 4 through 8 provide detailed reviews of the different APIs introduced with Android Wear, including notifications, Wear UIs, communicating with mobile apps, voice interactions and location-based services.

Chapters 9, 10, and 11 describe building wearable applications and projects that include Android Wear.

Android Wear is an area that is in constant motion, much like Android was in its infancy. Therefore, the technologies used for developing Android Wear change often. We used the latest versions, but you may see some discrepancies with your development environment.

HOW THIS BOOK IS STRUCTURED

The chapters stand on their own and therefore can be read in any order. But we've structured this book in a logical fashion to help introduce the wearable novice to this exciting field.

The more experienced Android developer who has a good understanding of wearable technology can start with Chapter 4. That chapter and the ones after it discuss the details of the new Wear-specific APIs using basic examples.

When you've read Chapters 4 through 8, you're ready to start developing your own application ideas. Or you can get inspiration from the sample projects in Chapters 9 through 11.

WHAT YOU NEED TO USE THIS BOOK

To run the examples found in this book, you must have a working development environment for Android Wear. For this you need an updated Java Development Kit, the SDK, and the development tools. It's highly recommended that you download Android Studio, because it contains the Wear-specific helper dialogs and makes development easier.

The examples in this book have been tested on Windows, Mac, and Linux computers. You can download the tools for all three systems from the Android website.

Although a real Android Wear device is recommended, you do not need one for most of the examples in this book. You may find that the examples in Chapters 9, 10, and 11 do not work well on an emulator.

The source code for the examples is available for download from the Wrox website at:

www.wrox.com/go/androidwearables

CONVENTIONS

To help you get the most from the text and keep track of what's happening, this book uses a number of conventions.

> **WARNING** *Warnings hold important, not-to-be-forgotten information that is relevant to the surrounding text.*

> **NOTE** *This books also contains notes, tips, hints, tricks, and asides to the current discussion.*

As for styles in the text:

➤ We *highlight* new terms and important words when we introduce them.

➤ We show keyboard strokes like this: Ctrl+A.

➤ We show filenames, URLs, and code within the text like this: persistence.properties.

➤ We present code in two different ways:

```
We use a monofont type with no highlighting for most code examples.
We use bold to emphasize code that is particularly important in the present
context or to show changes from a previous code snippet.
```

SOURCE CODE

As you work through the examples in this book, you can type in all the code manually, or you can use the accompanying source code files. All the source code used in this book is available for download at www.wrox.com. The code downloads for this book are on the Download Code tab at:

www.wrox.com/go/androidwearables

Chapters that have companion code files are noted as such at the beginning of the chapter. The code files are named according to the code listing numbers throughout the chapter.

You can also search for this book at www.wrox.com by ISBN (this book's ISBN is 978-1-1189-8685-1) to find the code. A complete list of code downloads for all current Wrox books is available at www.wrox.com/dynamic/books/download.aspx.

> **NOTE** *Because many books have similar titles, you may find it easiest to search by ISBN.*

Most of the code on www.wrox.com is compressed in a .zip file, a .rar archive, or a similar archive format appropriate to the platform. After you download the code, just decompress it with an appropriate decompression tool. Alternatively, you can go to the main Wrox code download page at www.wrox.com/dynamic/books/download.aspx to see the code available for this book and all other Wrox books.

ERRATA

We have made every effort to ensure that the text and code contain no errors. However, no one is perfect, and mistakes do occur. If you find an error in one of our books, such as a misspelling or faulty piece of code, we would be grateful for your feedback. By sending in errata, you may save another reader hours of frustration, and at the same time, you will help us provide even higher-quality information.

To find the errata page for this book, go to,

    www.wrox.com/go/androidwearables

and click the Errata link. On this page you can view all the errors that have been submitted for this book and posted by Wrox editors.

If you don't spot "your" error on the book's errata page, go to www.wrox.com/contact/techsupport.shtml and complete the form there to send us the error you found. We'll check the information and, if appropriate, post a message to the book's errata page and fix the problem in subsequent editions.

P2P.WROX.COM

For author and peer discussion, join the P2P forums at http://p2p.wrox.com. The forums are a web-based system for you to post messages about Wrox books and related technologies and to interact with other readers and technology users. The forums offer a subscription feature that e-mails you topics of interest when new posts are made to the forums. Wrox authors, editors, other industry experts, and your fellow readers are present on these forums. The forums will help you not only as you read this book, but also as you develop your own applications. To join the forums, follow these steps:

1. Go to http://p2p.wrox.com, and click the Register link.
2. Read the terms of use, and click Agree.

3. Complete the required information to join, as well as any optional information you want to provide, and click Submit.

4. You receive an e-mail describing how to verify your account and complete the joining process.

> **NOTE** *You can read messages in the forums without joining P2P, but to post messages, you must join.*

After you join, you can post new messages and respond to messages other users post. You can read messages at any time. If you would like to have new messages from a particular forum e-mailed to you, click the Subscribe to this Forum icon by the forum name in the forum listing.

For more information on how to use the Wrox P2P, read the P2P FAQs. You'll find answers to questions about how the forum software works, as well as answers to many common questions specific to P2P and Wrox books. To read the FAQs, click the FAQ link on any P2P page.

PART I
Concepts

1

Introduction to Android Wearables

THE WEARABLE REVOLUTION

Wearable technology is the next big thing in the world of connected devices. It is made of sensors and actuators so close to your skin that they can literally monitor your vital signs, with so much computing power they can make on-the-spot suggestions on health habits, so connected they can notify you about the important things to do today by mining data from your calendars and e-mails, and so ubiquitous they can remind you of tasks from your wrist, or overlaying information right in front of your eyes.

Wearables are small-yet-powerful computers that fit in your pocket or mounted on top of your glasses. They hang from a key ring, and your kids have them in their shoes to indicate the way back home via vibrations.

These concepts aren't science fiction, but are current technologies that allow for this and more. Lighter devices with smaller screens and different use patterns, like the smartwatches, increase battery life. One-touch user interfaces (also known as zero UIs) will help you navigate through complex menus in ways you never imagined.

As you will see later, there are different categories of wearables. Google has launched three different APIs exploring them: Wear for smartwatches, Fit for fitness devices, and Glass for their smart glasses. Not all companies are jumping into these three categories in the same way, and not all of them are willing to commit to open standards.

The terms "wearable technology," "wearable devices," and "wearables" all refer to electronic technologies or computers that are incorporated into items of clothing and accessories which can comfortably be worn on the body.

KIANA TEHRANI AND ANDREW MICHAEL

The latest shift in technology is getting everyone within the tech industry to notice wearables. The preceding definition of what a "wearable" actually is leaves much room for interpretation. It fits everything from iPod controls embedded in the sleeve of your ski jacket to intelligent shoes that tell you which direction to turn when you reach an intersection.

The wearable revolution we are witnessing is the result of an extreme miniaturization of technology, the development of more efficient batteries, and the broadening of the communication infrastructure. Thanks to advancements in technology, we can carry in our pocket as much computing power as a stationary computer had in the late 1990s. And because of communication capabilities, we can take advantage of much more computing power residing in the cloud.

In this post-PC era, many people will never use a computer in the same way we are using it to write this book or to develop applications for the devices described in it. The next generation might access the web from only mobile browsers. A Bloomberg report from 2010 predicted that 36 percent of Indonesia's population would be able to access the Internet in four years, with only 15 percent doing so from a PC. Many of them will start using wearable computers as peripherals to their mobile devices in a much more natural way than we can anticipate.

This chapter gives you an overview of the history of wearable computing and also introduces current trends. Wearables are becoming part of our everyday lives, harvesting data about our whereabouts, health condition, and interests. This chapter introduces the ecosystem of wearables and explains how the different pieces of the puzzle connect.

DISMANTLING THE COMPUTER: THE CYBORG DREAM

Steve Mann, a tenured professor in the Department of Electrical and Computer Engineering at the University of Toronto, is considered the father of wearable computing. Mann, a PhD from MIT, has published more than 200 articles and books on topics ranging from algorithms for the treatment and analysis of digital images to his everyday experiences as a cyborg.

In the early years of wearable computing, Mann used to dismantle computers and make them into wearable devices. He realized that the interaction paradigm for the wearable computer couldn't be the same as that for a PC. Imagine yourself carrying the motherboard and hard drive in different vest pockets, with the heavy battery hanging from your belt, and, as input mechanisms, a camera with added intelligence and a one-button interface. For output, you would wear goggles reproducing an augmented reality (AR) version of audible feedback and what the camera films.

Because he needed to place the technology closer to the body, Mann had to further evolve user interfaces (UIs). Early computers used a command-line interface (CLI); later they used a graphical user interface (GUI). Mann coined the term natural user interface (NUI), which would become the bread and butter of many human-computer interaction (HCI) researchers.

Mann started by taking apart a computer and looking at ways to enhance human cognition by adding layers of AR to what he was seeing. Along with learning how technology could merge with the body without being intrusive, he invented one-button interaction, wearable glasses, and other things that are the essence of contemporary wearable devices.

SOFTWARE EVERYWHERE

Neil Harbisson was the first person allowed to pose for his passport photo as a cyborg. In 2004 he was implanted with a device called an eyeborg, which translates colors into auditory stimuli to make up for his color blindness. The eyeborg lets him perceive ultraviolet and infrared light, which the human eye cannot see. From a purely software point of view, this is very different from the general-purpose computer Mann designed. It is instead a single-purpose machine: It enhances Harbisson's eyesight.

In the same way that a multipurpose machine lets you change the software for a different use, Harbisson believes that what makes him a cyborg is actually the software. He explained in a 2011 interview that it's not the union between the eyeborg and his head that converts him into a cyborg, but the union between the software and his brain.

When it comes to code, most wearable devices follow the model of embedded computing. The weapon of choice is usually nano-power processors with specially written software to command the devices' sensors, actuators, and communication. This is closer to Harbisson's augmentation machine than to Mann's general-purpose machine.

This book is all about software in wearables. We will look at which hooks different devices offer to connect them to Android phones and tablets. Some devices, like the original Sony SmartWatch, have a specific software development kit (SDK) to create applications to be executed in the device and offer an API to allow the watch to talk to an app in a phone. Most of the health bracelets on the market (such as Fitbit, Jawbone, and Nike FuelBand) follow this approach. Sometimes they don't even offer an open API of any kind to allow developers to write their own applications for the device.

Other gadgets, such as Google Glass and the Vuzix glasses (discussed in the section "Glasses"), run their own flavor of Android's OS. In that case, developers are supposed to create applications that can take advantage of the device's specific features.

We can see two main lines of work for developers. Either they write specific apps for devices that run the Android OS, or they write apps on phones and tablets that talk to APIs offered by a certain gadget via Bluetooth or WiFi.

In an attempt to standardize the API between gadgets and the Android OS, Google is launching Android Wear, a version of the Android OS specific to the wearable realm. The idea is to create an operating system for wearables that can easily sync with other Android devices. In that way, Android Wear will offer app developers a simple way to operate rich notifications more than a full-fledged system to create applications.

Some players that came earlier than others to the wearable business—like Sony—seemed uninterested in Android Wear, and were willing to stick with its own SDK to create apps for its SmartWatch ecosystem. But with the arrival of Wear 2.0, the second revision of Android Wear, Sony announced that the 3rd generation of the Sony SmartWatch will also be an Android Wear device.

FASHION IS MORE THAN SKI JACKETS

Wearables offer more than computation power and technical advancement. They are objects we carry with us every day, and they are fashion statements. To succeed as products, wearables have to be desirable. Fashion plays a huge role in this.

The reason for the title of this section is that one of the first applications in the field of wearable technology was an iPod controller embedded in the sleeve of ski jackets. These so-called soft buttons are a version of the tactile switches on many contemporary printed circuit boards (PCBs). They are made of soft materials such as conductive fabrics, foams, and threads.

Fashion, as a creative endeavor, is extremely important in the development of wearable technology as we know it today. Beyond the simplistic approach offered by the ski jacket, we find designers trying to look at conductive materials with different eyes. A good example is the collaboration between Hussein Chalayan and Moritz Waldemeyer in 2007 that resulted in a collection of robotic dresses. These dresses use electromechanical parts to change their shape as the models walk down the runway. Making small, on-the-fly modifications to the surface of one garment in particular causes it to change into the style of a dress from the '40s, '50s, or '60s. These dresses are designed for the runway, not mainstream consumers, but they show how far it is possible to push technology, embedding motors and sensors in minimal space.

A piece closer to the topic of this book is the T-shirt OS project created by design couple CuteCircuit. Their T-shirt with 1,024 pixels arranged in a 32-by-32 grid can display nearly anything. It can show notifications coming from your mobile device, and it also has an accelerometer, camera, microphone, and speakers. You control it using a mobile phone app. Besides shirts, CuteCircuit have embedded LEDs in dresses and the leather jackets musical group U2 wore during one of their tours.

In a sense, the garment is an extension of the phone, almost like a smartwatch. But because of its wearable nature, it makes people behave differently. Suppose your T-shirt displayed your heart rate as you walked down the street. Don't you think you would try to move in a way that your shirt wouldn't tell others how out of shape you are?

Another aspect of wearable technology is that, because we wear it all the time, we forget we are carrying it, and then it makes us change our behavior and relationships to others.

Currently, only the garments mentioned here run Android or Android Wear. For the time being, the kinds of gadgets we can focus on are smartwatches, glasses, bracelets, and other activity trackers. But we believe that in a couple of years, more products like CuteCircuit's T-shirt will make it to the mass market, and we will see people programming their clothes.

FITNESS

Activity bands, or fitness trackers, are devices that help you keep track of your daily physical effort. Typically, these devices communicate with your phone via an app that lets you do basic configuration on them and load data from the specific sensors on the band. Examples of this category of device are Fitbit, SmartBand, Jawbone, Fuel, and Misfit. And new products continue to be created.

Most of these bands work through APIs, a series of callback functions that can be accessed via Bluetooth to get information about the sensors, alarms, and so on. The way software is constructed within these activity bands makes them pretty simple.

A strict definition of wearable computing requires the devices part of this categorization to be reprogrammable; they must be adjustable to different use scenarios. In other words, a wearable computer is a general-purpose machine that people wear close to their bodies. However, the definition has softened over time. New types of devices, such as activity bands, are not truly reprogrammable but offer APIs that let you use them as part of a bigger system.

One of the most direct applications of activity bands is improving health conditions, mostly on the preventive side of the issue. More complex sensors and smart uses of existing sensors such as accelerometers let you gather all sorts of information in an instant: temperature, pulse, blood pressure, galvanic skin resistance, steps walked in the last 24 hours. Even if no commercial band is yet ready to diagnose anything, the potential of the preventive-medicine applications of these wearables is endless.

TIME

Smartphones pushed watches out of our lives. The most basic function of the watch, showing the time, became superfluous when mobile phones included that function. During the last couple of years, technology manufacturers have realized that adding connectivity to the watch, thus making it a smart device, was the added value the watch needed to be hyped again.

We have seen how giants such as Samsung, LG, and Sony have started flooding the market with watches that are nothing but an extension of phones or tablets. Most smartwatches offer an interface to our cloud that doesn't require us to take something out of our pocket all the time.

Android Wear, the new SDK by Google, basically offers an easy way to create software for smartwatches from vendors that are ready to follow some specifications. Watches are powerful computational units, including touch screens, sensors, a microphone, and a camera. The production of software for each of these devices used to require downloading the respective SDK from the manufacturer and writing code for the device under the manufacturer's terms. Android Wear tries to make things easier for app developers, so that they need to deal with only a single way to write applications for watches.

EVERYTHING CAN BE HACKED

As mentioned earlier, smartwatches, activity bands, and other wearable garments correspond pretty well to the embedded computer model. In essence, they are a small computer running a special-state machine that allows them to run some sub-applications on top.

Considering that nowadays most development tools for microcontrollers offer open source equivalents, it is possible with a little effort to create alternative-state machines or even SDKs for a wearable device.

continues

continued

In the summer of 2013, Arduino Verkstad, the Swedish office of the Arduino open source project, was challenged by Sony's design office to hack the Sony SmartWatch version 1.

Thanks to some initial hints about the peripherals contained in the SmartWatch, the Arduino developers put together a version of their software tools to reprogram the SmartWatch. Figure 1-1 shows the SmartWatch running self-made code using the Arduino IDE.

Hacking is not the focus of this book. We want to focus on standard methods of producing code for Android wearables. We want to teach you how to create apps that can later be deployed in many devices at once.

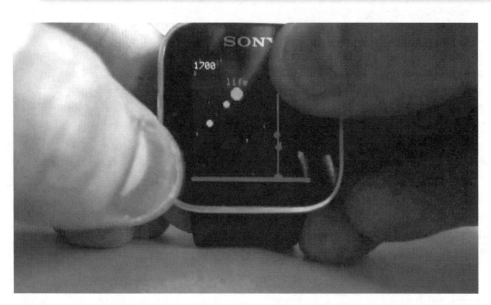

FIGURE 1-1: Sony SmartWatch v1 hacked to be programmed using the Arduino IDE by Arduino Verkstad (image by Asier Arranz)

GLASSES

Visual augmentation is probably the most interesting kind of wearable. It merges fields such as computer vision and augmented reality into something useful for everyday life.

In 1981, Steve Mann created the EyeTap. Worn in front of the eye, it acts as a camera to record what the wearer sees and also superimposes computer-generated imagery on the scene. This artifact is a true ancestor to Google Glass that has been through several iterations. It even comes in waterproof versions.

As a matter of fact, Mann is one of the main critics of the design of Google Glass. As the inventor of one of the most advanced display technologies, he has created his own opportunities by becoming chief scientist of Meta, a company developing a wearable computer with 15 times the display size of Google Glass. He is pushing for a new HCI paradigm called zero user interface (ZUI), in which the user will be able to interact manually with holograms projected by the AR glasses. It looks as though these SpaceGlasses will not run Android but their own 3D operating system.

In a way, this seems to be the paradigm of 3D interaction with interpersonal space. Oblong, another U.S.-based company, has been developing an NUI in which users interact with the space around them and have their actions recorded by an array of infrared cameras. John Underkoffler, chief scientist at Oblong, designed the famous UI for the movie *Minority Report*. Oblong's first series of products are based on *Minority Report*'s UI and use state-of-the-art technology. However, as stated on Oblong's website, its main discovery is not the gestural interface, a type of NUI, but a new type of OS that can support multiple users, devices, and screens and that is strongly networked.

A detailed discussion of the products from Meta and Oblong is outside the scope of this book. Although they are technologically interesting, their realization doesn't involve Android. However, they are worth mentioning because they explore the same kinds of user interfaces we will develop in this book using other devices that connect to the Android OS.

A third company, Vuzix, has created a set of AR glasses that support features that are relevant to us: notifications, cue cards, and voice commands. (These three topics are covered in Part II, and the Vuzix glasses are covered in Chapter 11.) This piece of technology is an Android device in itself. Unlike other smart devices that run their own embedded code and offer Android-friendly APIs to Android phones and tablets, the Vuzix glasses run Android as their OS. It is possible to create applications for them using standard development tools.

Project Glass is Google's approach to this category of wearable devices. It's currently unclear whether Glass will become part of the Android Wear SDK or if it will remain a separate Android device, just as the Vuzix glasses do. Glass and Vuzix are similar, although Vuzix focuses much more on the professional application sector, with its suite of AR applications.

SUMMARY

This chapter has introduced the concept of wearable computing. It included a basic timeline of how the field has evolved over the last 30 years.

Wearable computing is a not-so-new computing paradigm that is about to transform the way we use technology as much as tablets did only a few years ago. Technology is now mature enough to force smart devices out of our pockets and onto our wrists in the form of bracelets and watches, or in front of our eyes as augmented reality glasses.

Technology vendors look at ways to make money out these new trends and offer new chipsets, APIs, innovative battery systems, etc. Google has figured out how to incorporate a lot of the research done in the field over the last decades into a series of software APIs to explore the communication between wearable devices and their surroundings in an easy way. This book will be mostly about getting different devices we carry on us to talk to each other, share information and trigger events.

Chapter 2 will invite you to look into the current paradigm of connected devices: the Internet of Things.

RECOMMENDED READING

Interview with Neil Harbisson at `http://www.ara.cat/premium/societat/No-blancs-negres-tots-taronges_0_411558847.html`

Moritz Waldemeyer online portfolio at `http://www.waldemeyer.com/hussein-chalayan-111-robotic-dresses`

Kiana Tehrani and Andrew Michael. "Wearable Technology and Wearable Devices: Everything You Need to Know." March 2014. *Wearable Devices Magazine*, WearableDevices.com.

The Jakarta Globe website at `http://www.thejakartaglobe.com/archive/internet-users-in-indonesia-to-triple-by-2015-report/`

The Internet of Things

WHAT'S IN THIS CHAPTER?

- ➤ The Internet of Things and the Internet of Everything
- ➤ The 2020 vision: 50 billion connected devices
- ➤ Categories of devices

The *Internet of Things* (IoT) is a concept that states that everything that *can* be connected *will* be connected. This computing paradigm evolved from both ubiquitous computing and pervasive computing. IoT has three basic rules:

1. *Connectivity is key*. Objects will connect to each other either directly or through other devices using many technologies. Connectivity implies *over the air* (OTA) updates. Suppose a series of embedded devices in the home required firmware upgrades. If they didn't follow an OTA strategy, you would have to run a cable to each one to change their basic configuration.

2. Each device will have a *unique identifier* to distinguish it from others via software. Technologies such as IPv6 allow devices to have searchable identifiers (IP numbers) within the group, but internally the devices need a unique identifier to distinguish them from the rest.

3. Communication devices should provide *encryption* so that users can hide information as needed.

HOW WEARABLES RELATE TO IoT

Wearable devices play an important role in this vision. They are IoT devices in the sense that they are always connected to the Internet, even if it is through a device such as a phone or tablet. Many people already own or plan to purchase wearables for fitness or medical reasons.

Eventually wearables will become essential work tools. Imagine factory workers wearing bracelets that report their vital statistics as well as information about their environment. Imagine workers processing food using gloves that analyze the food's quality at the chemical level. Imagine police officers wearing glasses that display information about passing vehicles. Imagine nurses wearing rings that monitor patients' blood pressure and upload the information to their chart.

> **WARNING** *The future of wearables goes hand in hand with the future of IoT. You could say that one informs the other and that one couldn't exist without the other.*

THE PROMISE OF CONNECTIVITY

In February 2011, communications technology company Ericsson published a whitepaper describing the company's vision of 50 billion connected devices by the year 2020. Connected technology will reach many fields. It will cause more disruption in some fields than others, as shown in Figure 2-1. This figure is based on a memo from Cisco presented in January 2014.

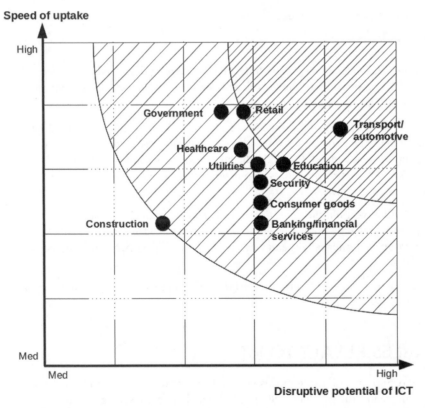

FIGURE 2-1: Information and communication technologies (ICT) disruptive potential versus speed of uptake by field of application (source: Cisco)

Connectivity is one of the most important topics discussed in this book. Only networks that allow for exponential scalability will make it possible. The decrease in cost per gigabyte of transfer is also an important factor in the explosion of connected technologies. This vision goes beyond smart living and game technologies. It can be applied to every field of our lives.

Cisco's Vision

Ericsson's report was the beginning of a war of numbers. Cisco estimated that by 2020 the world population will be 7.6 billion, compared to the current 7.2 billion. Ericsson suggested that, despite this relatively slow population growth, the number of connected devices will increase from the current 12.5 billion to as many as 50 billion. If you think about simple home devices that can be connected, such as electric meters and smoke alarms, 12.5 billion sounds too small.

An online article in *Time* magazine after the global consumer electronics and consumer technology trade show CES 2014 elaborated on Cisco's vision. It looked at market researcher IDC, which projects that by 2020, 220 billion connected devices will be in use. Every company predicts a different number of connected devices because each company uses a different way to define "connected device."

We will say that a device is connected as soon as it can reach the Internet, even if it does so through a third party. In this way, your refrigerator, your car, your mobile phone, your garden sensor reporting soil moisture, and your activity band are all connected devices. They are technological tools that possess some computational power, that can connect to the Internet, and that can be used to read a sensor or control an actuator (or both).

Big Data

Big data refers to collections of data that are so large that they cannot be computed by traditional means. This could be due to the multiplicity of data sources to be compared or to the size of each one of the records. Here are some examples of big data:

- ➤ The location of every mobile phone in a certain country
- ➤ The collection of all Google searches for white Americans over 25 years of age
- ➤ What products of a certain brand are bought at supermarkets in Spain by customers younger than 40, cross-referenced with the location of the most commonly bought products in the store

All these cases can provide interesting sets of data that, when explored carefully, could become interesting from both a research and marketing point of view. But how are we meant to approach the problem of all of these data sets? How will we generate them? Who will curate that data, filter it, and make it available?

Cisco brings to the conversation the idea that the amount of data generated in this globally connected network, which some people call the *Internet of Everything* (IoE), will be so big that we will need distributed computation closer to the data sources. It will be virtually impossible to process all the data sent to the cloud. Think about the number of sensors and actuators in a car. It would be impossible for all the cars in the world to report all that data to the cloud. The systems will have more embedded intelligence and will share only meaningful data.

Silicon vendors such as Qualcomm, Atmel, Intel, Broadcom, ST, and Texas Instruments are trying to produce the best platforms to stay always on and always connected. Those handling the spectrum, such as AT&T, Telefonica, and Vodafone, have their own way of understanding where the value of IoT lies. The following sections discuss different applications of IoT beyond wearable computing.

CONNECTED DEVICES IN THE HOME

In the home, it makes sense to connect security and safety devices. An IP security camera that streams to the Internet, a smoke alarm, and a burglar alarm are perfect examples. Other examples include anything dedicated to measuring and accounting for how you use resources, such as your electric, water, and gas meters. They all have a clear application; being connected brings an added level of service. Other machines in your home also can benefit from being connected.

Suppose you buy an induction stove. This type of stove is probably the most complex piece of engineering in your kitchen. It contains multiple processors that regulate radio waves that heat metallic materials. Besides having all the typical intelligence of any device in the home, these appliances run small neural networks to, for example, determine whether the pot on the stove is made of steel or aluminum. The latter is much less efficient at transferring heat. Therefore, the stove will refuse to heat an aluminum pot. Many of these operations require dedicated microchips (ASICs) instead of general-purpose processors like the ones commanding your microwave. As a result, an induction stove ends up being more expensive than almost anything else in your kitchen.

Currently, the price of adding something as simple as a WiFi or Bluetooth modem to your stove is nothing compared to the appliance's cost. But other devices, such as a water heater or an inexpensive coffeemaker, are much less expensive, so the price of connecting them to the Internet might not be worth it. If there were a good reason to connect such appliances, we probably would have done so already.

The SandS project, which stands for social and smart, is a series of pilot projects undertaken by the European Commission in which intelligent home appliances connect to the Internet. The project, which started near the end of 2012, has brought together researchers from seven European institutions and companies, working to build connected washing machines, ovens, refrigerators, bread-baking machines, and other appliances.

If you need help programming your washing machine to remove a strawberry stain from a shirt, you can tell the system to look for appropriate cleaning "recipes" in the SandS cloud service. It translates a natural-language request such as "Remove strawberry stain from white shirt" into a piece of XML that gives you the best recipe for your specific machine. The program then is automatically downloaded to your machine, leaving it ready to run.

Another example is the more complex activity of baking. It is a long process that requires adjusting the temperature as you go, or the direction of the heat (from the top or bottom, with or without ventilation). Again, the technical "recipe" could be downloaded from the cloud to the oven.

This process is what the SandS project is experimenting with, and this is what the connected home could be like if the researchers behind the project succeed. However, remember that, even if your coffeemaker is connected to the Internet (see Figure 2-2), you still need to put in water and coffee grounds. And even if your washing machine downloads "recipes" from the cloud, you still need to put the clothes in.

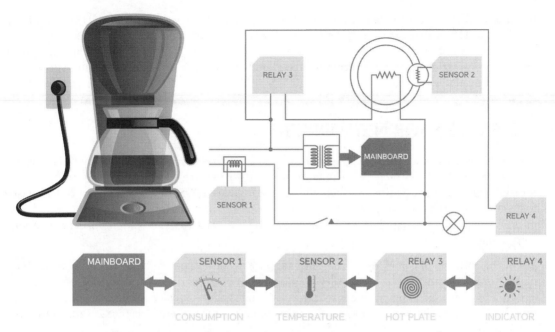

FIGURE 2-2: Connected coffeemaker for the SandS EU research project (source: Arduino)

CONNECTED DEVICES ON THE GO

What we call the *on the go* (OTG) category of IoT devices refers to devices that people can either wear or carry as they move. This group is composed of mostly small, lightweight gadgets that fit in our pockets. They are usually not connected directly to the Internet, but to our smartphones or tablets. Some of them are wearables, but that is not their defining characteristic.

OTG sensors are already common. They create small networks with your smartphone, mostly via Bluetooth. Examples include the famous Nike+® or any pedometer that tells your phone how far you've walked. There are also luggage tags that report whether your suitcase made it to the baggage claim area at the airport. Pacemakers that can be read via radio also fall into this category. Any ultraportable device that runs on batteries and acts as an extra input to your phone or tablet is an OTG device.

Information extracted from OTG devices can be shared via the Internet. Your health habits can be sent directly to your doctor. You may want to share your running records with friends living far away.

OTG actuators are still in their infancy. It isn't that technology isn't ready, but that we haven't really found a use for it. Some examples from the worlds of product and fashion design could be classified as OTG actuators. For example, a mini Segway for Android phones can transform your phone into a small, two-wheeled robot. T-shirts with flat LED displays pulse to the music sent by your tablet. Many of the new wearables, like some of the interactive rings announced during 2014, include nine-axis accelerometer sensors and tiny vibrators to give the users physical feedback.

Bluetooth and near field communication are the most relevant technologies in the OTG category of IoT devices. They create *piconets* of devices that move with you. In essence, each of us is like a small walking version of the Internet. As explained in the section "Cisco's Vision," our phones and tablets are the gateway to the Internet, making that small bubble of wireless sensor information floating around us available to others.

WIRELESS SENSOR NETWORKS

The OTG category describes the emergent field of technologies that aren't necessarily wearable but that are at least easily portable. A much more clearly defined category within IoT has been around for some time—the one dedicated to *wireless sensor networks* (WSNs). This field, which has existed for years, is devoted to creating smart networks that can be deployed quickly to monitor buildings, measure environmental data in farm fields, track farm animal activity, or simply collect data about your home.

The main characteristic of WSNs is that they use wireless technology to cover a certain area. One of their most relevant aspects is that they are meshed. In other words, it is possible to extend the network by simply adding new nodes to it. Information is automatically routed from one node to the next until it reaches the gateway that in turn connects to the Internet. Figure 2-3 illustrates this functionality.

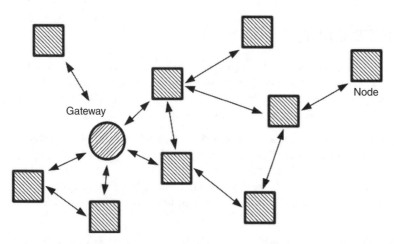

FIGURE 2-3: Mesh network architecture

A Scenario of Use of WSN

A typical WSN scenario is a network that monitors patients in a hospital. Most hospitals were built some time ago. Therefore, it is not easy to make these buildings "smart." A simple way to do so would be to install a WSN to monitor something like the room temperature in different areas, informing the building's maintenance staff if the heating or air-conditioning systems aren't working.

Another example would be to monitor patients to keep them from leaving their rooms when they shouldn't. All this information can be sent to a central system, where the data can be visualized. Deploying a network like this one the traditional way would be complicated. On the other hand, using WSN to cover the whole hospital would be as simple as adding sensors to the corridors and rooms. By doing so, you could build a mesh network that you can grow as much as needed.

As you can imagine, this way of transferring data does not support high speeds, because the data packages make multiple jumps between devices before reaching their destination. But it is good enough for scenarios like the ones described here.

Bluetooth Versus ZigBee

Both ZigBee and the latest version of Bluetooth can deploy mesh networks. Meshed networks have been implemented over WiFi, but not many vendors support it. ZigBee and Bluetooth were specifically designed with this "meshed network" scenario in mind.

ZigBee and Bluetooth operate in the same part of the open radio frequency spectrum (around 2.4GHz, a band where anyone can transmit without having to request special permissions from the authorities) and handle multiple channels in a similar way. Unlike WiFi, they take tiny portions of the spectrum and transmit for short periods of time. Then they jump to a different channel to continue transmitting there. This technique is called *frequency hopping* and allows technologies to be combined.

In this way, even if you have a WiFi network on 2.4GHz, you can also have a series of Bluetooth or ZigBee devices on the same portion of the spectrum. Bluetooth takes larger portions of the signal space but at lower energy averages, whereas ZigBee devices take smaller fractions of the spectrum but use more energy. The average interference of Bluetooth or ZigBee on WiFi can be cleaned easily via software. At the same time, the noise produced by WiFi on the others is too far below the threshold to be noticed.

Both ZigBee and Bluetooth are low-power techniques. Sensors running on either of these technologies can run on coin batteries for years if their refresh rate is low (a couple of times per minute).

Bluetooth has been around longer than ZigBee and is available in most mobile devices and laptops. This makes it likely to win in the long run. However, Bluetooth's mesh capabilities have only been available for about a year. This means that some companies have already invested in deploying ZigBee networks. Therefore, it is hard to know at this point which one will be used more in the future within WSNs.

One of the best possible uses of WSNs are smart cities, as described in the next section.

SMART CITIES

Most people live in cities, allowing them to share resources efficiently through infrastructure such as water utilities and highways. Infrastructure also helps residents get access to human resources such as doctors, education, and meeting other people for recreation.

What makes a city "smart" is its ability to connect the infrastructure to a network so that services can be created to better inform citizens about the availability of resources. An example is the public transportation system. If the buses report their locations, intelligent bus stops will know when the next bus is expected. Another example is detecting amounts of nighttime traffic to decide how many streetlights are needed to keep the streets safe while keeping energy consumption low. Rental cars could act as a moving sensor network to report traffic jams or even pollution levels.

As you can see, the possibilities are endless. The question with smart cities is whether data gathered by public systems should be made public. If it isn't, this is usually because sharing the data requires infrastructure. If the data is made public, individuals and companies could study it and use it to propose changes or new services.

SUMMARY

This chapter introduced the Internet of Things and the relationship of this field to wearable technology. You read about the vision of a connected future as interpreted by different companies. You learned terms such as the Internet of Everything, big data, and smart cities.

All of these topics are related in some way. For example, it is hard to imagine a scenario where you would have smart devices but not be part of a smart city infrastructure. The main vision to keep in mind is that there will be a network of automatically connected devices—this is part of IoT evolving from the Machine to Machine (M2M) business. At the same time there will be a network of personal devices that are connected, and the wearable devices fall within this category. It is like having a cloud of devices in parallel to a cloud of people.

The next chapter introduces the software tools (SDK) needed to write code for wearable devices running Android. Get closer to an Internet connection, because you will need to download some software!

RECOMMENDED READING

"More than 50 billion connected devices." Whitepaper by Ericsson. February 2011.
    http://david.cuartielles.com/files/2014/2011_Ericsson-More-than-50-billion-connected-devices.pdf
Tim Bajarin. "The next big thing for tech: the Internet of Everything." *Time*. January 13, 2014.
    http://time.com/539/the-next-big-thing-for-tech-the-internet-of-everything/

3

Platforms and Technology

WHAT'S IN THIS CHAPTER?

- ➤ Installing the Android Wear SDK
- ➤ Working with emulators and real devices
- ➤ Connecting the Android Wear Preview App to your Wear emulator
- ➤ Importing and running your first Android Wear project

WROX.COM CODE DOWNLOADS FOR THIS CHAPTER

The wrox.com code downloads for this chapter are found at www.wrox.com/go/androidwearables on the Download Code tab. The code is in the Chapter 3 download and the filename is Listing_3-1.gradle.

ANDROID WEAR

Android Wear is Google's attempt to bring order to a market that historically has been fairly scattered. Looking at recent releases in the smartwatch and wearables category for the mass market, you'll notice that most device manufacturers, such as Samsung and Sony, use proprietary tools and libraries. This puts third-party developers like you and me in an awkward position. We have to either support just one system, such as Samsung's Tizen, or build more-complex applications that use SDKs from multiple device vendors.

Most Android Wear devices are designed as an extension to a standard Android smartphone, providing new forms of interaction and more direct feedback from your Wear-enabled Android apps by using specially designed notifications and apps.

INSTALLING THE WEAR SDK

Before you can start developing for Android Wear you need to make sure your development environment is set up to support it. The following are requirements for developing for Android Wear:

➤ Android Studio, at least version 0.8.0, is almost a requirement when developing for Android Wear. Of course you can use other IDEs as well, but Android Studio comes with a set of Wear-specific tools and starter kits that make getting started with Wear a breeze.

➤ An Android SDK that has support for Android Wear; the first version that supports Wear is 4.4W (API 20).

➤ The Android Support Repository version 4 or version 13 (which happens to include the changes in version 4).

➤ A mobile phone running at least Android 4.3 (API 18).

You should also go ahead and install the appropriate Android Wear System Image, in most cases this is the Intel x86 Atom, and create an emulator. A good practice is creating at least two emulators, one for the rectangular screen and one of the circular screen.

WORKING WITH THE ANDROID WEAR EMULATOR

Android Wear comes in two screen configurations, rectangular and round. You should set up one emulator for each configuration. Go ahead and create an emulator for both the Round screen (Figure 3-1) and the Rectangular screen (Figure 3-2).

FIGURE 3-1: Round Android Wear emulator

FIGURE 3-2: Square Android Wear emulator

> **NOTE** *It's a good idea to keep the hardware keyboard available for Wear emulators even though a real device has no keyboard. The idea is to mimic the voice input that is unavailable on an emulator.*

Because the Android Wear device is an extension to your normal Android device, you also need a connection to your normal phone to receive notifications. Google's Android Wear App connects to your Emulator.

You can download the Android Wear App from `https://play.google.com/store/apps/details?id=com.google.android.wearable.app`.

After you've installed the Android Wear App, you see the screen shown in Figure 3-3.

The Android Wear App works as a bridge between your real Android device (or a second emulator). Setting up a connection between your real Android device and the Wear emulator is easy, but you need some familiarity with the Android Debug Bridge (ADB).

FIGURE 3-3: The Android Wear App screen

ANDROID DEBUG BRIDGE

If you're using Android Studio on a Windows machine, you should find your adb tool under C:\Users*username*\AppData\Local\Android\android-studio\sdk\ platform-tools. To access the adb tool, follow these steps:

1. Open the command prompt.

2. Type **cd C:\Users*username*\AppData\Local\Android\android-studio\sdk\ platform-tools.**

3. If you run adb.exe, you should see a list of possible commands.

4. To list all the connected Android devices (including Wear emulators), run adb .exe devices.

To get better acquainted with the ADB command set, visit `http://developer` `.android.com/tools/help/adb.html#commandsummary` and review all the commands. This chapter focuses on the `port forward` command.

To set up the connection, follow these steps:

1. Start your Wear emulator.

2. Connect your Android device to your computer.

3. Verify that both devices are properly connected to the ADB by typing **adb devices**.

4. With the Android Wear App running, type **adb -d forward tcp:5601 tcp:5601.**

5. Press the Connect button on your Android device. If the connection is successful, you should see the screen shown in Figure 3-4.

WORKING WITH A REAL WEAR-ENABLED DEVICE

There are currently two different Android Wear devices available: the LG G Watch and the Samsung Gear Live, and they both use square screens. Motorola has announced a round watch which will be available soon.

NOTE *You can see all the available devices at* `https://play.google.com/` `store/devices`. *If you don't see any Wear devices on that website, don't be alarmed—Android Wear is still only available in a limited number of countries. Sweden, where I live, is not on that list yet.*

FIGURE 3-4: Successful connection between the Wear emulator and an Android device

To work with either of these devices during development you first need to pair the Wear device to your Android Phone. But first, lets become a developer!

1. Tap the screen on your Wear device once.

2. Instead of asking Wear to do something for you, scroll down to select **Settings**.

3. Again, scroll down and select **About**.

4. Find the row that says **Build number** and start tapping it like your life depended on it.

5. Eventually (after 7 or so taps) the device surrenders to your persistence and grants you developer permissions.

6. Go back by swiping to the right, then open the **Developer options**.

7. Enable both **ADB debugging** and **Debug over Bluetooth**.

Now it's time to connect your Wear device to your development environment; when you connect your Wear device to your computer you'll get the typical "Allow USB Debugging" dialog, but you'll get it on the phone instead of the Wear device, as shown in Figure 3-5.

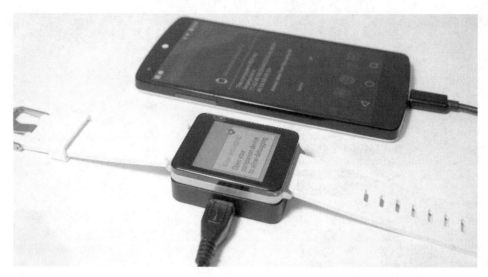

FIGURE 3-5: Allow USB Debugging on Wear

With the Wear connected and having allowed USB debugging for your computer, you're all set! Just remember to select the correct device when uploading apps from Android Studio—you shouldn't install mobile apps on the Wear, or Wear apps on the mobile.

If you prefer to limit the amount of cables on your desk you can choose to debug over Bluetooth. Enable the setting for Bluetooth debugging in your Wear companion app.

1. With the companion app open, open the menu and select Settings.

2. Connect the mobile phone to your computer over ADB and enter **adb forward tcp:4444 localabstract:/adb-hub** and **adb connect localhost:4444.**

3. If you were successful the status in the companion app should list both the host and the target as connected.

KICK-STARTING YOUR WEAR DEVELOPMENT

Now that your Android device and your Wear emulator are connected, your next step is diving straight into development.

Download the sample applications for Android 4.4W using the SDK Manager. Let's install one of them to test the connection using the following steps:

1. Find your Android SDK location.

2. Navigate to the samples directory.

3. You should find an application called Recipe Assistant, which is a simple app providing step-by-step cooking instructions. Remember the path.

4. Open Android Studio.

5. Select File ➤ Import Project.

6. Navigate to the RecipeAssistant project folder, and click OK.

7. Select Run ➤ Run.

> **WARNING** *When importing the sample application, you may have issues regarding a wrong version of Android Build Tools. To fix this, open the* `build` `.gradle` *file and change the* `buildToolsVersion` *to the build tools installed on your system. For me this is 20.*

If everything goes well, you should see the view shown in Figure 3-6.

Select one of the recipes. You should see the walk-through start on your Wear emulator. Figure 3-7 shows the first step in the beef brisket chili recipe.

A common misconception when developing Wear apps is that you should install apps straight to the Wear device. This is not the intended workflow when developing for Wear. You should avoid installing apps straight to the emulator, because the result may cause undocumented behavior.

DISTRIBUTING WEAR APPS ON GOOGLE PLAY

Installing apps directly on the Wear device is only available when developing through the ADB tool. If you want to distribute an app for Wear devices on Google Play, you will need to package this inside a standard app.

When installing an app with a wearable component from Google Play, the app is automatically pushed from your phone to the Wear device.

FIGURE 3-6: Recipe Assistant

FIGURE 3-7: Steps 1 through 3 of preparing beef brisket chili

For this to work you need to package the application properly before you release it on Google Play. The following steps quickly describe how to package your Wear app for Google Play:

1. Open the mobile `build.gradle` file and add the `wearApp` to your dependencies, if it's not already added (code filename: `Listing_3-1.gradle`).

LISTING 3-1: Adding the wearApp dependency

```
{
    compile fileTree(dir: 'libs', include: ['*.jar'])
    wearApp project(':wear')
    compile 'com.google.android.gms:play-services-wearable: +
}
```

2. From the Build menu, select Generate Signed APK and follow the instructions.

3. Log into your Google Play Developer Console and publish your new Wear-enabled app.

SUMMARY

This chapter has introduced the Android Wear system, its ideas, and its position within the Android ecosystem. You also kick-started your development by creating a Wear emulator and connected it to the Android Wear App. If you have a real Wear device, you probably also tested connecting that device to your real phone. You finished this chapter by installing your first Android Wear-enabled app to your phone and making sure it connected to your emulator properly. Finally, you looked at special considerations for distributing Wear-enabled applications on Google Play.

Coming up in Chapter 4, you'll learn about building notifications tailored specifically for Android Wear.

PART II
Basic Building Blocks

Notifications on Small Screens

WHAT'S IN THIS CHAPTER?

- ➤ Notification overview
- ➤ How to build notifications
- ➤ How to build Wear-enabled notifications

WROX.COM CODE DOWNLOADS FOR THIS CHAPTER

The wrox.com code downloads for this chapter are found at www.wrox.com/go/androidwearables on the Download Code tab. The code is in the Chapter 4 download and the files are named according to the Listing numbers noted throughout the chapter.

ABOUT NOTIFICATIONS

Notifications are one of two essential ways of telling the user what is currently going on. Since its release, Android has seen the Notifications grow from displaying simple messages onscreen to becoming core interactive elements of the Android app.

Starting somewhere around Android version 4.1, you could build large custom notifications with multiple optional actions that link directly to your underlying application. This makes interactions with your application short and simple. Your users no longer need to open your application to interact with it.

With Android Wear, Google has kept this strategy. Notifications play a large role in how the user interacts with your application, through what Google calls microinteractions. Each notification in Wear can consist of many subnotifications called pages. Each page is a small part of the whole notification experience, such as information, interactions, or feedback.

Pre-Wear Notification API

Since Android 3.0 (or API 11, depending on your preference), you have been able to use the `Notification.Builder` class to create notifications. Table 4-1 describes some of the options used most frequently to build notifications for Android handheld devices.

TABLE 4-1: Notification Options for Handheld Devices

METHOD	DESCRIPTION	REQUIRED?
`setContent(RemoteViews)`	Selects a custom layout object using a `RemoteViews` object, similar to a normal `View` object. In Wear these `RemoteViews` simply show the notification's content, ignoring any custom layout you may have created.	No
`setContentInfo(CharSequence)`	Conveys a minor piece of extra information, such as the number of new messages in your app	No
`setContentIntent(CharSequence)`	Sets a specific action to take when the user clicks your notification	No
`setContentText(CharSequence)`	Sets a detailed message for your notification	No
`setContentTitle(CharSequence)`	Sets the title of your notification	No
`setLargeIcon(Bitmap)`	Sets a large icon for your notification	No
`setPriority(int)`	Sets the priority for your notification and tells the system how to display or not display your notification	No
`setSmallIcon(int)`	Sets the small icon that should be displayed in the status bar when your notification is active	Yes
`setStyle(Notification.Style)`	Let's you further customize your notification with predefined styles	No
`setWhen(long)`	Sets a timestamp that is important to your notification, such as when a message was sent or received	No

As the table shows, only one item is required to show a notification—the small icon. Everything else is (technically) optional. A message and title are highly recommended. The same requirements are true for Wear notifications.

Wear Notifications

Notifications on Wear devices work much like notifications on handheld devices. However, instead of presenting all notifications in a `ListView`, Wear takes a different approach. It uses a `GridView`, as shown in Figure 4-1. In this Wear startup tutorial, each card or notification takes up a full screen. Navigating the grid is easy using swipe gestures.

FIGURE 4-1: Wear navigation

As Figure 4-1 also shows, each notification can consist of multiple messages. In Android each of these is called a page and can be either purely informative or an action the user can take from the watch. Examples include instantly replying to a message and opening an application on the handheld device.

Wear notifications use the standard API but also add extra features for Wear-specific notifications through the `NotificationCompat.WearableExtender` class. Table 4-2 describes some of the new wearable notification features.

TABLE 4-2: New Features in Wear Notifications

METHOD	DESCRIPTION	REQUIRED?
`addAction(Action)`	Lets you add actions that are accessible only on Wear devices	No
`addPage(Notification)`	Adds extra pages to your main notification	No
`setBackground(Bitmap)`	Lets you add a background image for the Wear notification	No
`setContentAction(int)`	Lets you link an action directly to the notification	No
`setGravity(int)`	Sets the notification's location on the screen	No
`setHintHideIcon(boolean)`	Hides the application icon for the Wear notification	No

You use wearable features by instantiating the `WearableExtender` class, applying each feature you want your notification to have, and then extending the `Notification.Builder` instance with the new Wear-specific features. This process is detailed in Listing 4-1.

LISTING 4-1: Applying Wear-specific features to your notifications

```
NotificationCompat.WearableExtender wearFeatures = new
    NotificationCompat.WearableExtender();

Notification notification = new NotificationCompat.Builder(this)
    .setContentTitle("My first notification")
    .setContentText("My first wear notification!")
    .extend(wearFeatures)
    .build();
```

You'll read more details on all the new wearable features as you progress through the chapter, building all the different types of notifications available in Wear.

BUILDING NOTIFICATIONS

There is no tangible difference between displaying notifications in Android Mobile or Android Wear. The only difference is the classes you use. As you know, you can use the `NotificationManager` class to launch notifications on handheld devices. However, it is always recommended that you use `NotificationManagerCompat` instead of the `NotificationManager` as it provides support on older devices as well as receives bug-fixes and updates that don't require firmware updates. Since Wear introduces new features for the Wear-enabled notifications, you need to use the `NotificationsManagerCompat` class found in the support libraries (v4 or above). Listing 4-2 shows how to acquire the handle for the new `NotificationManagerCompat` service.

LISTING 4-2: Storing a reference to the `NotificationManager`

```
public class MyActivity extends Activity {

    NotificationManagerCompat mNotificationManager;

    @Override
    protected void onCreate(Bundle savedInstanceState) {
      super.onCreate(savedInstanceState);
      setContentView(R.layout.activity_my);

      mNotificationManager = NotificationManagerCompat.from(this);
    }
}
```

To show a notification you use the `notify(int, Notification)` method from the `NotificationManagerCompat` handle, passing a unique ID (and optionally a tag as well) of the notification you want to show and the notification itself. Listing 4-3 and Listing 4-4 demonstrate this.

LISTING 4-3: Showing a notification with a unique identifier

```
int NOTIFICATION_ID = 1;

mNotificationManager.notify(NOTIFICATION_ID, notification);
```

LISTING 4-4: Showing a notification with a unique tag and identifier

```
String NOTIFICATION_TAG = "My notification";
int NOTIFICATION_ID = 1;

mNotificationManager.notify(NOTIFICATION_TAG, NOTIFICATION_ID, notification);
```

If you need different kinds of notifications in your app, use multiple notification identifiers to separate each notification. If you're using tags, it's sufficient to change the combination of tag and identifier.

The Simple Notification

Building the most basic notification is easy. You pass the notification's core information to the `NotificationCompat.Builder` class and launch it using `NotificationManagerCompat`. The core information is the small icon, the content title, and the content text. Anything more is just icing on the cake.

> **NOTE** *You'll notice that in the examples I tend to use the standard Android icons. I do this because it's easy and the launcher icon* ic_launcher.png *is automatically created for you when you make a new project in both Eclipse and Android Studio. When building a "live" project, you should use a custom icon that follows the icon design guidelines. For example, the notification icon must be 24-by-24 dp and use only flat white color. Read more about the icon design guidelines at* http://developer.android.com/design/style/iconography .html.

Listing 4-5 shows how to build the simple notification.

LISTING 4-5: The basic notification

```
Notification notification = new NotificationCompat.Builder(this)
    .setSmallIcon(R.drawable.wrox_logo_small)
    .setContentTitle("My notification")
    .setContentText("My first wear notification!")
    .build();
```

This notification is generally used to display short messages that never stack. It is not generally used to notify users about new e-mails or chat messages. Figure 4-2 shows the simple notification.

FIGURE 4-2: Basic text notification

> **WARNING** *If the notification doesn't show up on your device or emulator, be sure to enable notification access for Android Wear. On your mobile, open Settings and navigate to Sound & Notifications ➤ Notification Access and select Android Wear from the list.*
>
> *You need to have the Wear Companion app installed. You can find it at* https://play.google.com/store/apps/details?id=com.google.android .wearable.app. *You must be logged in to your Google Play account to access this app.*

Adding a Large Icon

Wear notifications draw the application's icon, defined in AndroidManifest.xml, in the upper-right corner of the notification. So far you've seen the standard droid icon being used. To change this to something more intriguing, you need to add a new icon to your application. Listing 4-6 shows how to add a custom icon to your manifest.

LISTING 4-6: Adding a custom icon to your Wear notifications

```xml
<?xml version="1.0" encoding="utf-8"?>
<manifest xmlns:android="http://schemas.android.com/apk/res/android"
          package="com.wrox.wear.chapter4">

  <application
    android:allowBackup="true"
    android:icon="@drawable/wrox_logo_big"
    android:label="@string/app_name"
    android:theme="@style/AppTheme">
    <activity
      android:name=".MyActivity"
      android:label="@string/app_name">
      <intent-filter>
        <action android:name="android.intent.action.MAIN"/>

        <category android:name="android.intent.category.LAUNCHER"/>
      </intent-filter>
    </activity>
  </application>
</manifest>
```

This example uses the Wrox logotype as the application icon, as shown in Figure 4-3. When selecting your icon, you should consider the Android design guidelines.

You may have noticed that the color changes when you switch the application icon. Wear does this automatically to adjust your notifications background if you haven't set it manually.

FIGURE 4-3: Using the Wrox logotype for Wear notifications

Big Text Notification

If you want to build a notification where a larger message is displayed, such as the first few lines of a chat message, use the NotificationCompat.BigTextStyle() class. This gives you the option of setting long text and a summary, as shown in Figure 4-4. Android automatically adjusts the amount of space for your notification. You may notice that the notification can grow larger than the space available on the tiny screen. Therefore, be careful not to build notifications that are too large.

Listing 4-7 shows how to use the BigTextStyle class for Wear notifications.

FIGURE 4-4: Big text notification

LISTING 4-7: Showing long text in a notification

```
NotificationCompat.Style style = new NotificationCompat.BigTextStyle()
    .setBigContentTitle("My big title")
    .setSummaryText("My summary")
```

continues

LISTING 4-7: *(continued)*

```
    .bigText("Lorem ipsum dolor sit amet, consectetur adipiscing elit. " +
        "Integer tristique fringilla neque ornare convallis. Sed aliquam, " +
        "diam in elementum aliquet, odio massa adipiscing ligula, " +
        "at pretium justo velit et arcu.");

Notification notification = new NotificationCompat.Builder(this)
    .setSmallIcon(R.drawable.wrox_logo_small)
    .setContentTitle("Content title")
    .setContentText("Content text")
    .setStyle(style)
    .build();
```

You probably noticed that the number of details in the notification don't change when the new style is applied. For example, the content text is overwritten by the `BigTextStyle` values. The summary is also hidden on the Wear device. However, on the mobile device these details remain visible, as shown in Figure 4-5. Wear hides as much information as possible to keep the notifications easy to read at a glance.

Don't forget to include this data when building your notifications. It is still used for large notifications that are collapsed on your mobile device, as shown in Figure 4-6.

FIGURE 4-5: Big text notification on mobile

FIGURE 4-6: Big text notification, collapsed

Big Picture Notification

Similar to the extended text notification, the large image notification uses a special style called `NotificationCompat.BigPictureStyle` to build. Figure 4-7 shows an example of the large image notification.

When building the large image notification, be sure to use an image that is the proper size. An image that is too small might not fill the entire notification space, and an image that is too big may take too long to load and cause your application to be unresponsive. On Wear devices the big picture is used as both a background and a new page for the notification. The summary is, again, not used on Wear devices but is displayed on mobile.

FIGURE 4-7: Big picture notification

Listing 4-8 shows how to build a simple notification with a large image.

LISTING 4-8: Including large images in notifications

```
NotificationCompat.Style style = new NotificationCompat.BigPictureStyle()
    .setBigContentTitle("Balloons!")
    .setSummaryText("My summary")
    .bigPicture(BitmapFactory.decodeResource(getResources(), R.drawable.balloons));

Notification notification = new NotificationCompat.Builder(this)
    .setSmallIcon(R.drawable.wrox_logo_small)
    .setContentTitle("Balloons!")
    .setContentText("Content text")
    .setStyle(style)
    .build();
```

You can achieve a similar effect in Wear only by using the WearableExtender feature setBackground(). The difference is that setting the background works with all notifications, not just the BigPictureStyle notification. Listing 4-9 shows how to do this.

LISTING 4-9: Setting the background for your notification

```
NotificationCompat.WearableExtender extender = new NotificationCompat
    .WearableExtender()
    .setBackground(BitmapFactory.decodeResource(getResources(),
        R.drawable.balloons));

Notification notification = new NotificationCompat.Builder(this)
    .setSmallIcon(R.drawable.wrox_logo_small)
    .setContentTitle("Background notification")
    .setContentText("Using a custom background for a normal notification")
    .extend(extender)
    .build();
```

Updating a Notification

When you want to update the information in a notification, you need the unique identifier and tag, depending on how you launched the notification. If the unique identifier already exists for your package, the system knows to update that notification. If the unique identifier doesn't exist, the system launches a new notification. Listing 4-10 shows how to create and update a simple notification.

LISTING 4-10: Updating a notification

```java
Notification notification = new NotificationCompat.Builder(this)
    .setSmallIcon(R.drawable.wrox_logo_small)
    .setContentTitle("A simple notification")
    .setContentText("A short text")
    .build();

mNotificationManager.notify(NOTIFICATION_ID, notification);

Handler handler = new Handler();
handler.postDelayed(new Runnable() {
  @Override
  public void run() {
    Notification updatedNotif = new NotificationCompat.Builder(MyActivity.this)
        .setSmallIcon(R.drawable.wrox_logo_small)
        .setContentTitle("A simple notification")
        .setContentText("An updated, slightly longer, text")
        .build();

    mNotificationManager.notify(NOTIFICATION_ID, updatedNotif);
  }
}, 5000);
```

This example creates a new notification and then launches it. Then it uses the feature `postDelayed()` in the handler to update the same notification after 5 seconds. Figure 4-8 shows the notification before and after the update.

FIGURE 4-8: Updating a notification

Adding Pages to Your Notifications

Pages are a core part of Wear notifications. These are notifications that exist to the right of the initial notification. They are visible only to the Wear device, so be sure to plan the content of each page carefully.

To build the multipage notification, you need a list of pages (actually, they're notifications, but they're called pages). Then you need the `WearableExtender` to add the list of pages to your notification. Listing 4-11 shows how to add multiple pages to a notification.

LISTIN 4-11: Adding multiple pages to your notification

```
List<Notification> pages = new ArrayList<Notification>();
for( int i = 1; i <= 3; i++ ){
  Notification notification = new NotificationCompat.Builder(this)
      .setContentTitle("Page " + i)
      .setContentText("Text for page " + i)
      .build();
  pages.add(notification);
}

NotificationCompat.WearableExtender extender = new NotificationCompat
    .WearableExtender()
    .addPages(pages);

Notification notification = new NotificationCompat.Builder(this)
    .setSmallIcon(R.drawable.wrox_logo_small)
    .setContentTitle("Multi page notification")
    .setContentText("This is the first of many pages")
    .extend(extender)
    .build();
```

Figure 4-9 shows the resulting notification structure.

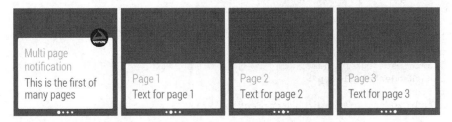

FIGURE 4-9: A simple multipage notification

Adding Actions to Your Notifications

When tapping a notification, you always have the option of performing an action, usually opening the application. Wear is no different. You have at least two ways to add actions to your notifications in Wear.

Adding a Standard Action

To have your notification, open the linked activity for your app on your mobile. Listing 4-12 shows how to add a standard action to your notification.

LISTING 4-12: Standard open action

```
Intent action = new Intent(this, MyActivity.class);

PendingIntent pendingIntent = PendingIntent.getActivity(this, 0, action,
    PendingIntent.FLAG_UPDATE_CURRENT);

Notification notification = new NotificationCompat.Builder(this)
    .setSmallIcon(R.drawable.wrox_logo_small)
    .setContentTitle("Standard action")
    .setContentText("This is the standard action notification")
    .setContentIntent(pendingIntent)
    .build();
```

Notice that the action appears on a separate action page on the Wear device, as shown in Figure 4-10.

You can avoid launching multiple instances of your activity by setting the launch mode to single top. Listing 4-13 shows how to edit your manifest to allow only one instance of your activity.

FIGURE 4-10: Adding a standard action to Wear notifications

LISTING 4-13: Setting activity launch mode to single top

```
...
<activity
  android:name=".MyActivity"
  android:label="@string/app_name"
  android:launchMode="singleTop">
  <intent-filter>
    <action android:name="android.intent.action.MAIN"/>

    <category android:name="android.intent.category.LAUNCHER"/>
  </intent-filter>
</activity>
...
```

> **NOTE** *Using the launch mode* single top *for your main activity as done here is not the recommended way of preventing the creation of multiple instances. Instead, you should create a separate* Activity *that handles whatever action your notification is pointing to, or deal with this in* Activity.onNewIntent().

Adding Multiple Actions

Adding more actions is just as easy as setting the content intent. The difference is you can set the desired icon and text to go along with them. Listing 4-14 shows how to add two actions—one to open the application, and another to open the standard dialer.

LISTING 4-14: Adding multiple actions

```
Intent act1 = new Intent(this, MyActivity.class);

PendingIntent pendingIntent1 = PendingIntent.getActivity(this, 0, act1,
    PendingIntent.FLAG_UPDATE_CURRENT);

Intent act2 = new Intent(Intent.ACTION_DIAL);

PendingIntent pendingIntent2 = PendingIntent.getActivity(this, 0,
    act2, PendingIntent.FLAG_UPDATE_CURRENT);

Notification notification = new NotificationCompat.Builder(this)
    .setSmallIcon(R.drawable.wrox_logo_small)
    .setContentTitle("Action notification")
    .setContentText("This notification has multiple actions")
    .addAction(R.drawable.wrox_logo_big, "Open app", pendingIntent1)
    .addAction(R.drawable.ic_launcher, "Call the droid", pendingIntent2)
    .build();
```

These actions display on both the handheld and the Wear device. If you want to add actions that display on only Wear devices, keep reading.

Adding Wear-Only Actions

To display actions on only the Wear device, you use the `WearableExtender` class and then add actions to the extender, as shown in Listing 4-15.

LISTING 4-15: Adding Wear-only actions

```
Intent act1 = new Intent(this, MyActivity.class);

PendingIntent pendingIntent1 = PendingIntent.getActivity(this, 0, act1,
    PendingIntent.FLAG_UPDATE_CURRENT);

NotificationCompat.Action action1 = new NotificationCompat.Action.Builder(R
    .drawable.wrox_logo_big, "Open app", pendingIntent1)
    .build();

Intent act2 = new Intent(Intent.ACTION_DIAL);

PendingIntent pendingIntent2 = PendingIntent.getActivity(this, 0,
    act2, PendingIntent.FLAG_UPDATE_CURRENT);

NotificationCompat.Action action2 = new NotificationCompat.Action.Builder(R
```

continues

LISTING 4-15: *(continued)*

```
        .drawable.ic_launcher, "Call the droid", pendingIntent2)
        .build();

    NotificationCompat.WearableExtender extender = new NotificationCompat
        .WearableExtender()
        .addAction(action1)
        .addAction(action2);

    Notification notification = new NotificationCompat.Builder(this)
        .setSmallIcon(R.drawable.wrox_logo_small)
        .setContentTitle("Action notification")
        .setContentText("This notification has wear-only actions")
        .extend(extender)
        .build();
```

The result is a normal notification on handheld devices. Wear devices, however, display actions, each on a separate page, as shown in Figure 4-11.

FIGURE 4-11: Standard actions on Wear notifications

Adding an Action without the Extra Page

In some cases you might want to add an action directly to your notification instead of creating another page for the action. You do this by defining which of the notification's actions should be connected directly to the notification content. This works for both normal actions and Wear-only actions.

Wear first checks to see if any wearable actions have been added. If so, it uses that list. If no wearable actions exist for the notification, Wear uses the standard list of actions. When the action is added to the notification content, Wear no longer creates an extra page for that action. Figure 4-12 shows the resulting notification.

FIGURE 4-12: Interactive Wear notification

Listing 4-16 shows how to add actions to the content of a Wear notification.

LISTING 4-16: Adding content action to Wear notifications

```
Intent act1 = new Intent(this, MyActivity.class);

PendingIntent pendingIntent1 = PendingIntent.getActivity(this, 0, act1,
    PendingIntent.FLAG_UPDATE_CURRENT);

Intent act2 = new Intent(Intent.ACTION_DIAL);

PendingIntent pendingIntent2 = PendingIntent.getActivity(this, 0,
    act2, PendingIntent.FLAG_UPDATE_CURRENT);

NotificationCompat.WearableExtender ext = new NotificationCompat
    .WearableExtender()
    .setContentAction(1);

Notification notification = new NotificationCompat.Builder(this)
    .setSmallIcon(R.drawable.wrox_logo_small)
    .setContentTitle("Action notification")
    .setContentText("This notification is clickable")
    .addAction(R.drawable.wrox_logo_big, "Open app", pendingIntent1)
    .addAction(R.drawable.ic_launcher, "Call the droid", pendingIntent2)
    .extend(ext)
    .build();
```

Extra Options

Wear includes other options that help you add detail to and customize your notifications.

Hiding the Application Icon

If you want to hide the application icon that usually is found in the top-right corner of your Wear notifications, you can do so using the `WearableExtender` class. Figure 4-13 shows a Wear notification without an icon.

FIGURE 4-13: Hidden icon for Wear notifications

Listing 4-17 shows how to hide the application icon.

LISTING 4-17: Hiding the application icon

```
NotificationCompat.WearableExtender extender = new NotificationCompat
    .WearableExtender()
    .setHintHideIcon(true);

Notification notification = new NotificationCompat.Builder(this)
    .setSmallIcon(R.drawable.wrox_logo_small)
    .setContentTitle("Hidden icon")
    .setContentText("The icon should be hidden on Wear")
    .extend(extender)
    .build();
```

Moving the Notification

You can also move the notification on the Wear screen using the `setGravity()` method. Table 4-3 shows the options for Wear notifications.

TABLE 4-3: Gravity Options for Wear Notifications

OPTION	DESCRIPTION
Gravity.BOTTOM	Places the notification at the bottom of its parent container. This is the default option.
Gravity.CENTER_VERTICAL	Places the notification in the middle of the parent container. This does not affect the horizontal alignment, because notifications always take up the full width of the Wear display.
Gravity.TOP	Places the notification at the top of its parent container.

Listing 4-18 shows how to set the gravity to `Gravity.TOP` for your notification.

LISTING 4-18: Moving the notification to the top

```
NotificationCompat.WearableExtender extender = new NotificationCompat
    .WearableExtender()
    .setGravity(Gravity.TOP);

Notification notification = new NotificationCompat.Builder(this)
    .setSmallIcon(R.drawable.wrox_logo_small)
    .setContentTitle("At the top")
    .setContentText("This should be placed at the top")
    .extend(extender)
    .build();
```

This example should give you a result similar to the one shown in Figure 4-14.

Setting the Scroll to the Bottom

For long text notifications, you can also let the user start reading at the end of the text instead of the beginning. Use the `setStartScrollBottom()` method, as shown in Listing 4-19. The default value is false.

FIGURE 4-14: A notification that sticks to the top of the screen

LISTING 4-19: Scrolling from the bottom

```
NotificationCompat.Style style = new NotificationCompat.BigTextStyle()
    .setBigContentTitle("My big title")
    .setSummaryText("My summary")
    .bigText("Lorem ipsum dolor sit amet, consectetur adipiscing elit. " +
        "Integer tristique fringilla neque ornare convallis. Sed aliquam, " +
        "diam in elementum aliquet, odio massa adipiscing ligula, " +
        "at pretium justo velit et arcu.");
```

```
NotificationCompat.WearableExtender extender = new NotificationCompat
    .WearableExtender()
    .setStartScrollBottom(true);

Notification notification = new NotificationCompat.Builder(this)
    .setSmallIcon(R.drawable.wrox_logo_small)
    .setContentTitle("Content title")
    .setContentText("Content text")
    .setStyle(style)
    .extend(extender)
    .build();
```

Removing a Notification

You have two ways to remove a notification. You can refer to the notification's unique identifier, or you can combine a unique identifier and a tag. Listing 4-20 and Listing 4-21 show how to remove notifications.

LISTING 4-20: Removing a notification by identifier

```
mNotificationManager.cancel(NOTIFICATION_ID);
```

LISTING 4-21: Removing a notification by tag and identifier

```
mNotificationManager.cancel(NOTIFICATION_TAG, NOTIFICATION_ID);
```

STACKING NOTIFICATIONS

You also can group notifications in a stack, rather than a collection of pages. This is useful when you have several similar notifications that don't necessarily belong to the same message. For example, if you have multiple e-mail conversations, you may want to stack the notifications to show that the user has multiple e-mails waiting.

Listing 4-22 shows how to create a simple stack of notifications.

LISTING 4-22: Stacking notifications

```
String MY_STACK = "my_custom_stack";

for( int i = 0; i < 3; i++ ){
   Notification notification = new NotificationCompat.Builder(this)
       .setSmallIcon(R.drawable.wrox_logo_small)
       .setContentTitle("Title " + i)
       .setContentText("Content for " + i)
       .setGroup(MY_STACK)
       .build();

   mNotificationManager.notify(NOTIFICATION_ID + i, notification);
}
```

This example creates three notifications in a loop; attaches them to the same group, called
MY_STACK; and then displays them one after the other. You can attach more notifications to the same
group later by reusing the stack name.

Remember that the notification identifier is unique to the notification.
If you use the same identifier for multiple notifications, the system
creates only one notification. In essence, the stack contains just one
notification if you don't change the identifier.

Figure 4-15 shows the resulting stack of notifications built by
Listing 4-22. The stack is sorted before the notification is launched.
If you want to use different sorting for your stack, you can use the
setSortKey() method, as shown in Listing 4-23.

FIGURE 4-15: Default sorted
stack of notifications

LISTING 4-23: Sorting the stacked notifications

```java
String MY_STACK = "my_custom_stack";

for( int i = 3; i >= 0; i-- ) {
    Notification notification = new NotificationCompat.Builder(this)
        .setSmallIcon(R.drawable.wrox_logo_small)
        .setContentTitle("Title " + i)
        .setContentText("Content for " + i)
        .setGroup(MY_STACK)
        .setSortKey(Integer.toString(i))
        .build();

    mNotificationManager.notify(NOTIFICATION_ID + i, notification);
}
```

This example sorts on the notification's index. However, you can use
any string to sort these notifications. You could use the sender's name
or the message's length, or perhaps a custom priority string for a
To-Do application. Figure 4-16 shows the stacked notifications sorted
by a custom key.

By default, the stacked notification doesn't appear on a normal
handheld device, so it's important that you provide a summary
notification to be displayed on those devices. Listing 4-24 shows a
simple summary notification.

FIGURE 4-16: Custom-sorted
stack of notifications

LISTING 4-24: Summary of stacked notifications

```java
String MY_STACK = "my_custom_stack";

int index = 0;

// Create summary notifications for handheld
NotificationCompat.InboxStyle list = new NotificationCompat.InboxStyle();
```

```
for( index = 1; index <= 3; index++ ){
   Notification notification = new NotificationCompat.Builder(this)
       .setSmallIcon(R.drawable.wrox_logo_small)
       .setContentTitle("Title " + index)
       .setContentText("Content for " + index)
       .setGroup(MY_STACK)
       .build();

   // For the handheld summary
   list.addLine("Title " + index);

   mNotificationManager.notify(NOTIFICATION_ID + index, notification);
}

list.setBigContentTitle(index + " new notifications")
    .setSummaryText("Many notifications...");


Notification stackedWithSummary = new NotificationCompat.Builder(this)
    .setSmallIcon(R.drawable.wrox_logo_small)
    .setContentTitle(index + " new notifications")
    .setLargeIcon(BitmapFactory.decodeResource(getResources(),
        R.drawable.wrox_logo_big))
    .setStyle(list)
    .setGroup(MY_STACK)
    .setGroupSummary(true)
    .build();
```

The resulting summary notification should look like Figure 4-17.

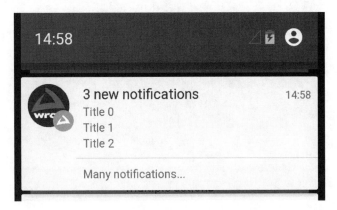

FIGURE 4-17: Handheld summary for stacked notifications

SUMMARY

This chapter has introduced the most commonly used notification features ported to a Wear device. You explored the new features that Wear has introduced to notifications, including Wear-specific actions, stacked notifications, and pages. You also learned that some of the standard notification APIs do not apply on Wear devices because of how users interact with the new form factor of Wear devices. You should keep this in mind when designing your applications experience—you probably want a similar look and feel for your app regardless of what kind of device the user has.

The next chapter dives further into the Wear APIs, discussing how to create custom Wear-enabled activities and applications.

RECOMMENDED READING

UI Patterns for Android Wear, http://developer.android.com/design/wear/patterns.html.

5

Developing Wear Apps

WROX.COM CODE DOWNLOADS FOR THIS CHAPTER

The wrox.com code downloads for this chapter are found at www.wrox.com/go/androidwearables on the Download Code tab. The code is in the Chapter 5 download and the filenames correspond to the code listing numbers noted throughout the chapter.

THE WEAR SDK

Unlike notifications, Wear apps behave (almost) like normal Android apps. They are built using a native SDK called Wear SDK, and they run in separate processes on the wearable device, making them completely standalone from your phone. Even though the behavior is similar, you should keep a few points in mind when developing apps for Wear.

Design Considerations

The first thing you should consider is the connectivity of your Wear device. It has no built-in connectivity options such as WiFi or USB for you to use when building your apps. Accessing the Internet on your Wear apps is impossible without an attached phone. But this is not a major problem, because you need to build a companion app (or, rather, a master app) for your Wear app. Without it you can't distribute your new Wear app on Google Play.

Google has published a number of general guidelines that you should keep in mind when creating your Wear app. For example, all Wear interactions should fall into one of two categories that Google calls suggest and demand. This means that everything found on Wear should be contextually connected. Everything you create for Wear, whether a notification or native running app, should interrupt only if absolutely necessary, and it should quickly provide a correct answer depending on the user's context.

A continuation of this rule of thumb is that you should create apps that don't require focused attention from your users. They should be able to quickly get the gist of what your app is trying to tell them. Or your apps should promptly suggest actions. Google calls this making the app *glanceable*.

A reasonable goal when creating Wear apps, or notifications, is that your users should interact with the device for only a few seconds. If they have to spend more time than that, your app could probably be more optimized and streamlined. Always try to focus your app on doing only one thing, and try to do that one thing as quickly as possible by helping the user in any way you can. For example, you can highlight the most plausible action.

A good strategy when helping your users complete actions quickly on such a small screen is to use simple gestures and interactions. Always avoid using complicated or detailed interactions. If users find your app difficult to interact with while on the move, you should redesign the user interface.

Wearable UI Library

With the introduction of Wear, Google added a number of new classes and UI widgets that help you create apps that follow Wear's design guidelines—and those of other small screens. Table 5-1 summarizes the new widgets.

All of these classes can be found in the `android.support.wearable.view` package.

TABLE 5-1: New Classes and UI Widgets in Wear

WIDGET NAME	DESCRIPTION
CardFragment	A fragment that holds a scrollable card. By default the card layout includes a title, descriptive text, and an optional icon. You can also build your own custom layout for this fragment.
CardFrame	Creates a frame with a white background and rounded corners for its contents. This is useful if you want your app to have a more detailed background—rather than the standard black—while the content remains readable.
CardScrollView	A container for one `CardFrame` that makes it scrollable. Appropriate for cards that hold more text.

WIDGET NAME	DESCRIPTION
CircledImageView	The standard widget for including images in Wear. It has an optional circle that you can give some style. An optional border on the circle supports progress. You can use it for countdowns in your app or to show progress.
ConfirmationActivity	A helper class for creating attractive animations as feedback for user actions.
CrossfadeDrawable	Lets you fade between two different drawables, creating a nice effect for your UI.
DelayedConfirmationView	A subclass to CircledImageview, with the added functionality of performing an action after a set period of time. Often used before you send an action to the mobile so that the user has time to cancel the action if needed.
DismissOverlayView	A simple view for adding interactions to dismiss your activity.
FragmentGridPagerAdapter	A page adapter that handles fragments. Used together with GridViewPager.
GridPagerAdapter	Another adapter for GridViewPager. This one is not for fragments.
GridViewPager	A two-dimensional grid of pages that allows the user to scroll in both dimensions.
InsetActivity	An activity with built-in support for detecting screen types on Wear devices. A good alternative to using WatchViewStub.
WatchViewStub	One of the most important additions in Wear. Use it to detect the device's screen type—round or square—and then load the correct layout for that device.
WearableListView	A list view implementation that is optimized for very small screens.
WearableListView.Adapter	An adapter for WearableListView. This is an abstract class, which means you need to subclass it when working with lists.

CREATING THE WEAR PROJECT

When working with Android Wear you need to have Android Studio version 0.8.0 or later installed to have access to the Wear-specific workflow and dialogs.

Follow these steps to create your new Android Wear project:

1. Click New Project in the Android Studio startup dialog, as shown in Figure 5-1.

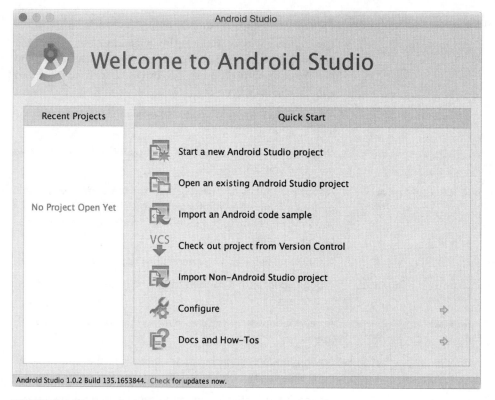

FIGURE 5-1: New project startup

2. Enter the correct information for your app. I'm calling mine "Chapter 5" and using the Company Domain wrox.wiley.com, as shown in Figure 5-2. Then click Next or press **Alt+N**.

3. As shown in Figure 5-3, select Phone and Tablet API 21. Also select Wear API 20. Then click Next.

4. Choose Blank Activity to add a blank activity to your mobile, as shown in Figure 5-4, and click Next twice to accept the default parameters.

5. Choose Blank Wear Activity, as shown in Figure 5-5. By default this is a standard activity with WatchViewStub as the main layout file. Click Next.

6. Notice in Figure 5-6 that Android Studio creates two layouts, **round_activity_my** and **rect_activity_my**. Leave them as they are for now. To create your new Mobile + Wear app, click Finish.

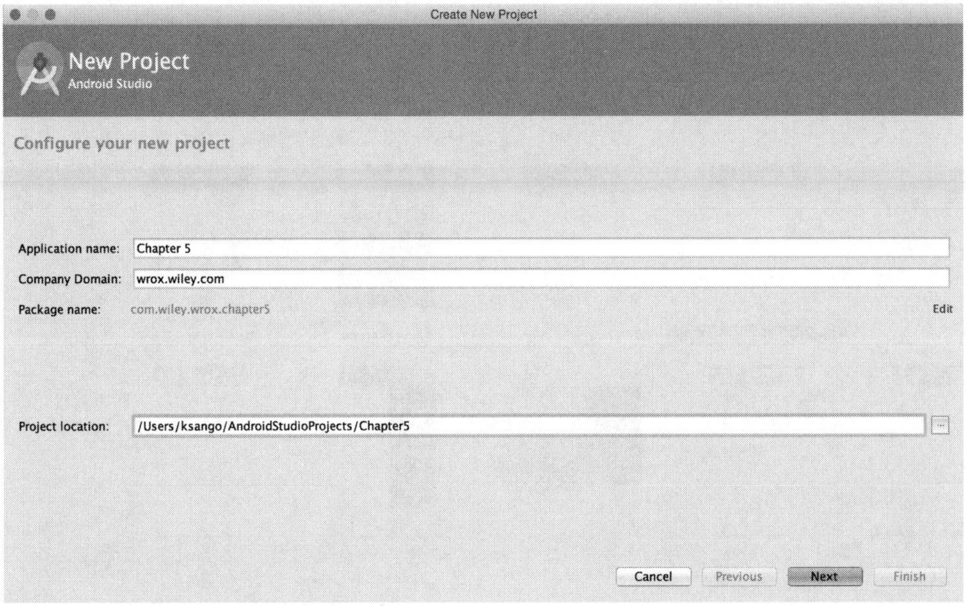

FIGURE 5-2: Entering project information

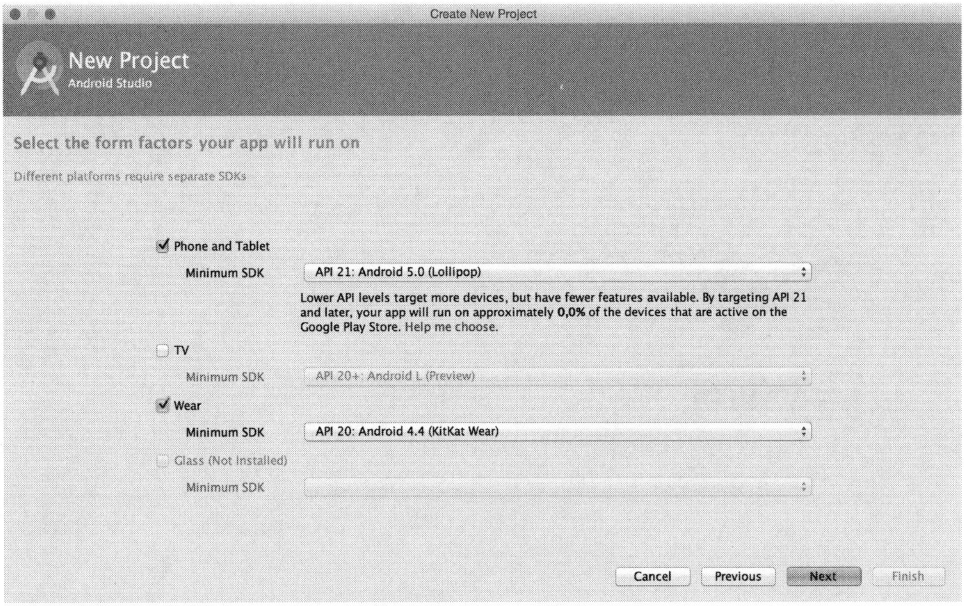

FIGURE 5-3: Select form factors and API levels for your app

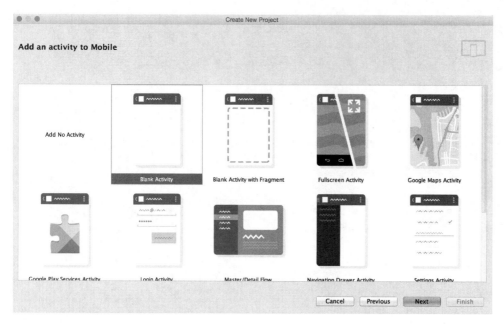

FIGURE 5-4: Add a blank phone activity

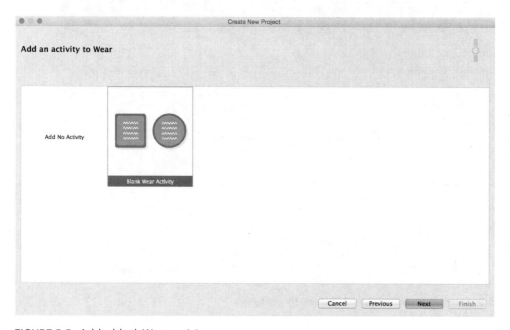

FIGURE 5-5: Add a blank Wear activity

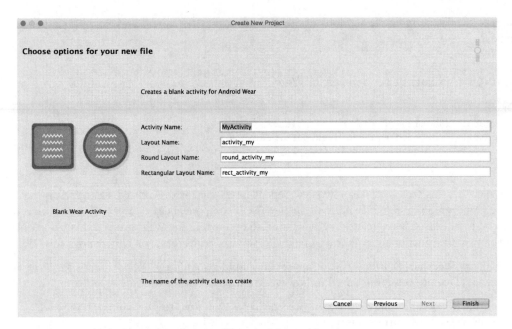

FIGURE 5-6: Edit the properties for your Wear activity and layouts

You should now have an Android Studio project that has two application structures within it called *mobile* and *wear*. Let's review some of the news introduced by Android Wear in the project.

Editing the Gradle Files

Open the mobile gradle file and scroll down to the dependencies. They should look something like Listing 5-1.

LISTING 5-1: Project dependencies for mobile

```
dependencies {
    compile fileTree(dir: 'libs', include: ['*.jar'])
    wearApp project(':wear')
    compile 'com.google.android.gms:play-services-wearable:+'
}
```

Notice the dependencies. These two lines are not present in normal Android app projects. The first line specifies that this particular Android app has a Wear component that is located in the wear folder.

The second line includes the Google Play services repository as part of the project. This part is optional. You may remove it if you don't plan on using any of the new Wear-specific features such as data sync between the two devices.

If you open the Wear gradle file and look at the dependencies, they should look something like Listing 5-2.

LISTING 5-2: Project dependencies for Wear

```
dependencies {
  compile fileTree(dir: 'libs', include: ['*.jar'])
  compile 'com.google.android.support:wearable:+'
  compile 'com.google.android.gms:play-services-wearable:+'
}
```

You'll notice that this project also has two new dependencies specific to Android Wear. First is the wearable support repository, which adds all the new Wear components (see Table 5-1) to the project. The second is the play services repository, which is also optional in the Wear project. If you don't plan on using any of the functionalities in the Google Play services repository, you may remove this line.

To use the new Wear notifications in your apps, you should also add the support repository to your dependencies. This project doesn't need it, however, so leave it out for now.

Since Android Wear comes in two different screen shapes, you need to plan your app for both shapes using at least two different layouts.

Loading Layouts

You have two ways to load the correct layout in Android Wear projects. The default method is to use a normal activity and load a layout with `WatchViewStub`. The second way is to use `InsetActivity`.

Using WatchViewStub

`WatchViewStub` is a smart UI widget that can detect the device's screen shape. Listing 5-3 shows the default main layout. Notice the attributes called `rectLayout` and `roundLayout`.

LISTING 5-3: Selecting different layouts for different shapes

```xml
<?xml version="1.0" encoding="utf-8"?>
<android.support.wearable.view.WatchViewStub
  xmlns:android="http://schemas.android.com/apk/res/android"
  xmlns:app="http://schemas.android.com/apk/res-auto"
  xmlns:tools="http://schemas.android.com/tools"
  android:id=@+id/watch_view_stub"
  android:layout_width="match_parent"
  android:layout_height="match_parent"
  app:rectLayout="@layout/rect_activity_my"
  app:roundLayout="@layout/round_activity_my"
  tools:context=".MyActivity"
  tools:deviceIds="wear">
</android.support.wearable.view.WatchViewStub>
```

The attributes found in the tools namespace are merely for convenience and helping you when you design the app. They are stripped when the application is packaged.

TOOLS NAMESPACE

For more information on using the tools attributes, see `http://tools.android` `.com/tech-docs/tools-attributes`.

When you design your actual layouts, you should always use the same components. It's critical to use identical ids when you work with `WatchViewStub`.

To get a reference to a UI widget in your layout, you listen for the `onLayoutInflated` event on the `WatchViewStub` root. Listing 5-4 shows how to add the listener.

LISTING 5-4: Listening for the onLayoutInflated event

```
@Override
protected void onCreate(Bundle savedInstanceState) {
  super.onCreate(savedInstanceState);
  setContentView(R.layout.activity_my);
  final WatchViewStub stub = (WatchViewStub) findViewById(R.id.watch_view_stub);
  stub.setOnLayoutInflatedListener(new WatchViewStub.OnLayoutInflatedListener() {
    @Override
    public void onLayoutInflated(WatchViewStub stub) {
    }
  });
}
```

When you've attached the listener, you can safely load references to the UI widgets, as shown in Listing 5-5.

LISTING 5-5: Loading references to your UI widgets

```
Button mButton;

@Override
protected void onCreate(Bundle savedInstanceState) {
  super.onCreate(savedInstanceState);
  setContentView(R.layout.activity_my);
  final WatchViewStub stub = (WatchViewStub) findViewById(R.id.watch_view_stub);
  stub.setOnLayoutInflatedListener(new WatchViewStub.OnLayoutInflatedListener() {
    @Override
    public void onLayoutInflated(WatchViewStub stub) {
      mButton = (Button) stub.findViewById(R.id.button);
    }
  });
}
```

This example shows the importance of having identical ids in the layouts for round screens and rectangular screens. The alternative way of loading layouts in Wear is a bit more lenient when it comes to ids.

Using InsetActivity

When using InsetActivity, you don't need the extra initial layout component, WatchViewStub. Instead of selecting the correct layout in XML, you load the correct layout directly in your activity. Listing 5-6 shows how to create InsetActivity.

LISTING 5-6: Creating InsetActivity

```
public class MyActivity extends InsetActivity {

    @Override
    protected void onCreate(Bundle savedInstanceState) {
        super.onCreate(savedInstanceState);
    }

    @Override
    public void onReadyForContent() {
        if( isRound() ){
            setContentView(R.layout.round_activity_my);
        }else{
            setContentView(R.layout.rect_activity_my);
        }
    }
}
```

The benefit of InsetActivity is that you may use completely different layouts for different screens. You don't need to make sure that they match in widgets or widget ids.

The biggest catch of InsetActivity is the loading of the content view. It must be loaded in the life-cycle method onReadyForContent(). Only in this method does the app know with certainty which screen type the device has. You may then load the correct layout depending on the type of screen the device has—round or rectangular. Using the isRound() method, you can select the correct layout to load as content view.

Loading references in InsetActivity is identical to loading references in any normal Android app. Using findViewById() in the activity, as shown in Listing 5-7, lets you load the correct widget. You're not required to use identical ids, unlike with WatchViewStub. But doing so is recommended so that you avoid duplicate code.

LISTING 5-7: Loading views with different ids depending on layout

```
public class MyActivity extends InsetActivity {

    private TextView rectText, roundText;
```

```
    @Override
    protected void onCreate(Bundle savedInstanceState) {
      super.onCreate(savedInstanceState);
    }

    @Override
    public void onReadyForContent() {
      if( isRound() ){
        setContentView(R.layout.round_activity_my);
        rectText = (TextView) findViewById(R.id.rectText);
      }else{
        setContentView(R.layout.rect_activity_my);
        roundText = (TextView) findViewById(R.id.roundText);
      }
    }
  }
}
```

I prefer to use a third method for loading the user interface to keep the life-cycle method clean. Doing so also ensures that the two screen types present the same information and enable the same interactions. Listing 5-8 shows how I usually organize my `InsetActivity`.

LISTING 5-8: Loading the user interface in a separate method

```
public class MyActivity extends InsetActivity {

  private TextView mTextView;

  @Override
  protected void onCreate(Bundle savedInstanceState) {
    super.onCreate(savedInstanceState);
  }

  @Override
  public void onReadyForContent() {
    if( isRound() ){
      setContentView(R.layout.round_activity_my);
    }else{
      setContentView(R.layout.rect_activity_my);
    }
    loadUi();
  }

  private void loadUi() {
    mTextView = (TextView) findViewById(R.id.myText);
    mTextView.setText("Hello InsetActivity");
  }
}
```

Figure 5-7 shows the application running on both screen types.

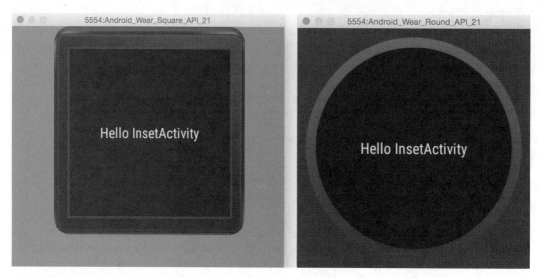

FIGURE 5-7: InsetActivity running on both screen types

Another cool function that `InsetActivity` provides is the exit button. Tapping the screen displays a typical exit application button, as shown in Figure 5-8.

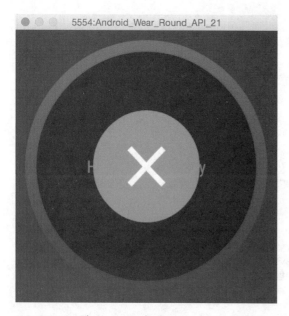

FIGURE 5-8: The exit app button as shown on a round device

Now that you know about some of the basic differences between the Wear app and the mobile app in terms of project structure, let's explore Wear's user interface widgets.

BUILDING THE USER INTERFACE

When working with Wear-specific UI widgets, it's important to add another namespace to your layouts. Without it, adding Wear attributes to views would be impossible. Listing 5-9 shows how to add the Wear namespace.

LISTING 5-9: Adding the XML namespace for Wear

```xml
<?xml version="1.0" encoding="utf-8"?>
<RelativeLayout
  xmlns:android="http://schemas.android.com/apk/res/android"
  xmlns:tools="http://schemas.android.com/tools"
  xmlns:wear="http://schemas.android.com/apk/res-auto"
  android:layout_width="match_parent"
  android:layout_height="match_parent"
  android:orientation="vertical"
  tools:context=".MyActivity"
  tools:deviceIds="wear_square">
  ...
</RelativeLayout>
```

Adding Text to Your User Interface

Working with text in Android Wear isn't so different from normal Android apps. Technically speaking, it's not the text component that changes; it's how you should design apps containing text in Wear that changes. Remember that context is important to both notifications and apps. Most often the context is provided with a visual background image and an application icon. Presenting textual information over an image may become a bit messy. Therefore, we strongly recommend that you use a frame of some sort that makes the text more legible.

Luckily Google provides several new classes for dealing with this problem—`CardFrame`, `CardScrollView`, and `CardFragment`.

CardFrame

The most basic of the three components for displaying text, `CardFrame` is a simple white card with rounded edges and an optional icon. Listing 5-10 shows how to wrap a simple `TextView` within a `CardFrame`.

LISTING 5-10: Adding a CardFrame to your layout

```xml
<android.support.wearable.view.CardFrame
  android:layout_width="wrap_content"
  android:layout_height="wrap_content"
  android:id="@+id/view"
```

continues

LISTING 5-10: *(continued)*

```
      android:layout_centerVertical="true"
      android:layout_centerHorizontal="true">

    <TextView
      android:layout_width="wrap_content"
      android:layout_height="wrap_content"
      android:text="R.strings.newtext"
      android:id="@+id/myText"
      android:layout_centerVertical="true"
      android:layout_centerHorizontal="true"/>

  </android.support.wearable.view.CardFrame>
```

The result is a simple frame around our `TextView`, as shown in Figure 5-9. It has rounded corners and a drop shadow, which is difficult to see in these figures. I promise it's there.

`CardFrame` doesn't give you many other options when it comes to customizing your UI. This is where `CardScrollView` comes in handy.

CardScrollView

`CardScrollView` is basically a container for a single `CardFrame` with the added option of adding scroll functionality to the card in two directions, up and down. You also can set the card's anchor edge to either top or bottom.

`CardScrollView` can hold only one `CardFrame` at a time, as shown in Listing 5-11.

FIGURE 5-9: CardFrame

LISTING 5-11: The CardScrollView layout

```
<android.support.wearable.view.CardScrollView
  android:layout_width="wrap_content"
  android:layout_height="wrap_content"
  android:id="@+id/myScrollView"
  android:layout_centerVertical="true"
  android:layout_centerHorizontal="true">

  <android.support.wearable.view.CardFrame
    android:layout_width="wrap_content"
    android:layout_height="wrap_content"
    android:id="@+id/myCardFrame"
    android:layout_centerVertical="true"
    android:layout_centerHorizontal="true">

    <TextView
```

```
    android:layout_width="wrap_content"
    android:layout_height="wrap_content"
    android:text="@string/lipsum"
    android:textColor="#000"
    android:id="@+id/myText"
    android:layout_centerVertical="true"
    android:layout_centerHorizontal="true"/>

  </android.support.wearable.view.CardFrame>
</android.support.wearable.view.CardScrollView>
```

Table 5-2 lists the properties you can change for CardScrollView. None of these parameters can be set in XML.

TABLE 5-2: CardScrollView Properties

PROPERTY	DESCRIPTION	METHOD
Expansion enabled	Allows or disallows CardFrame from being taller than the screen height.	setExpansionEnabled(Boolean)
Expansion direction	The direction in which the child CardFrame expands. When the card is taller than the screen, this edge is also faded to indicate that it is scrollable.	setExpansionDirection(int) This value can be either CardFrame.EXPAND_UP or CardFrame.EXPAND_DOWN
Expansion factor	Sets the expansion factor.	setExpansionFactor(float)
Card gravity	Sets the edge that the CardFrame child anchors to when the content is shorter than the screen's height.	setCardGravity(int) This value can be either Gravity.TOP or Gravity.BOTTOM

CardFragment

CardFragment is the best option for displaying text (or any other framed content, for that matter) on Wear devices. It combines CardFrame and CardScrollView and includes an icon as well.

CardFragment comes with two handy static builder methods. If the default layout doesn't suit your needs, you can simply extend CardFragment and load your own layout. Listing 5-12 shows how to create a simple card using the builder methods.

LISTING 5-12: Building a card using CardFragment builder methods

```
CardFragment myCard = CardFragment.create("My card", "A longer description",
    R.drawable.ic_launcher);

getFragmentManager().beginTransaction().replace(R.id.container, myCard,
    "myCard").commit();
```

Because this is a fragment, you need to adjust your layout slightly to create a container for your CardFragment. Figure 5-10 shows the resulting simple card.

FIGURE 5-10: The basic CardFragment

Using your own custom layout for the `CardFragment` class is simple. Just extend the `CardFragment` class and override the `onCreateContentView()` method. Listing 5-13 shows our custom card layout with three `TextViews`.

LISTING 5-13: The custom card layout

```xml
<?xml version="1.0" encoding="utf-8"?>
<LinearLayout
  xmlns:android="http://schemas.android.com/apk/res/android"
  android:layout_width="match_parent"
  android:layout_height="match_parent"
  android:orientation="vertical">

  <TextView
    android:layout_width="wrap_content"
    android:layout_height="wrap_content"
    android:textAppearance="?android:attr/textAppearanceLarge"
    android:text="Large Text"
    android:id="@+id/textView1"/>

  <TextView
    android:layout_width="wrap_content"
    android:layout_height="wrap_content"
    android:textAppearance="?android:attr/textAppearanceMedium"
```

```
          android:text="Medium Text"
          android:id="@+id/textView2"
          />

     <TextView
        android:layout_width="wrap_content"
        android:layout_height="wrap_content"
        android:textAppearance="?android:attr/textAppearanceSmall"
        android:text="Small Text"
        android:id="@+id/textView3"/>
   </LinearLayout>
```

Listing 5-14 shows how to load this custom layout in our own card class.

LISTING 5-14: Loading the custom layout in our custom card

```
public class MyCard extends CardFragment {

  TextView mTextView1, mTextView2, mTextView3;

  @Override
  public View onCreateContentView(LayoutInflater inflater, ViewGroup container,
                                  Bundle savedInstanceState) {
    View root = inflater.inflate(R.layout.custom_card, container, false);

    mTextView1 = (TextView) root.findViewById(R.id.textView1);
    mTextView2 = (TextView) root.findViewById(R.id.textView2);
    mTextView3 = (TextView) root.findViewById(R.id.textView3);

    return root;
  }
}
```

Showing this custom card is as easy as loading your custom fragment into the container, as shown in Listing 5-15.

LISTING 5-15: Loading the custom card fragment

```
MyCard myCard = new MyCard();

getFragmentManager().beginTransaction().replace(R.id.container, myCard,
    "myCard").commit();
```

Figure 5-11 shows the resulting card.

FIGURE 5-11: The custom CardFragment

Table 5-3 shows some of the available properties for `CardFragment`.

TABLE 5-3: CardFragment Properties

PROPERTY	DESCRIPTION
Scroll position	With the methods `scrollToTop()` and `scrollToBottom()` you can scroll the card contents to the very top and very bottom of the card.
Card gravity	Sets the card's anchor edge. Can be either `Gravity.TOP` or `Gravity.BOTTOM`.
Expansion direction	Selects in which direction the card expands. Can be either `CardFragment.EXPAND_UP` or `CardFragment.EXPAND_DOWN`.
Expansion state	With the method `setExpansionEnabled()`, you can allow or disallow the expansion for this `CardFragment`.
Expansion factor	Sets the card's allowed height. It's adjusted in multiples of the parent container. 1.5 means that `CardFragment` will be at most 1.5 times the height of its container.

Displaying Images

Images in Android Wear are used slightly differently than in normal Android apps. I like to categorize them into two groups: context images and action images.

Context images are your backgrounds; they provide context for the card currently displayed. It could be a photo of a contact who just sent you a message. Action images are part of the interactions in Wear. All action images in Wear are loaded with the new `CircledImageView`, which has special properties related to Wear user interfaces.

Loading a Static Image

The simplest image to load in Wear is the static image. Listing 5-16 is the simplest example of the image with a circled background.

LISTING 5-16: The basic CircledImageView

```xml
<?xml version="1.0" encoding="utf-8"?>

<RelativeLayout
  xmlns:android="http://schemas.android.com/apk/res/android"
  xmlns:wear="http://schemas.android.com/apk/res-auto"
  android:layout_width="match_parent"
  android:layout_height="match_parent">

  <android.support.wearable.view.CircledImageView
    android:layout_width="wrap_content"
    android:layout_height="wrap_content"
    android:id="@+id/view"
    android:layout_centerVertical="true"
    android:layout_centerHorizontal="true"
    android:src="@drawable/ic_launcher"
    wear:circle_radius="50dp"
    wear:circle_color="#f063c7"/>

</RelativeLayout>
```

This layout should render a result similar to that shown in Figure 5-12.

FIGURE 5-12: The basic CircledImageView

Adding a Progress Update

With the simple images in Wear, you need to use the limited amount of space wisely. A neat thing about `CircledImageView` is the optional progress bar—or countdown timer, depending on how you use it. Imagine a download is under way, and you want to show it on the watch's user interface. You'd probably create an `AsyncTask`, and, in the `onProgressUpdate()` method, you'd update the progress of `CircledImageView`, as shown in Figure 5-13.

To build the progress bar shown in Figure 5-13, you start by setting the color and weight of the circle border, as shown in Listing 5-17.

FIGURE 5-13: The progress bar at 60%

LISTING 5-17: Setting the border information

```xml
<?xml version="1.0" encoding="utf-8"?>

<RelativeLayout
  xmlns:android="http://schemas.android.com/apk/res/android"
  xmlns:wear="http://schemas.android.com/apk/res-auto"
  android:layout_width="match_parent"
  android:layout_height="match_parent">

  <android.support.wearable.view.CircledImageView
    android:layout_width="wrap_content"
    android:layout_height="wrap_content"
    android:id="@+id/circledImageView"
    android:layout_centerVertical="true"
    android:layout_centerHorizontal="true"
    android:src="@drawable/ic_launcher"
    wear:circle_radius="50dp"
    wear:circle_color="#f063c7"
    wear:circle_border_color="#00cc99"
    wear:circle_border_width="10dp"/>

</RelativeLayout>
```

To update the progress bar, you use the `setProgress()` method, as shown in Listing 5-18. The example isn't quite as complex as the scenario presented earlier, but it should give you a good idea of how to work with the circular progress bar.

LISTING 5-18: Enabling the progress bar

```java
CircledImageView mCircledImageView = (CircledImageView) findViewById(R.id
    .circledImageView);
mCircledImageView.setProgress(0.6f);
```

Table 5-4 lists all the possible attributes for the `CircledImageView` class.

TABLE 5-4: CircledImageView Attributes

XML ATTRIBUTE	DESCRIPTION
circle_color	Defines the circle's background color. In the layout file you can use normal RGB values. In Java you use the Color class. This property is required if you want the circle background to be displayed.
circle_radius	Sets the size of the background circle. Without it the circle is invisible.
circle_border_color	Sets the border's color. The circle's border is also the optional progress bar.
circle_border_width	Set the border's stroke weight. This is required if you want the border to show.
circle_padding	Sets the border's padding.

Handling Lists in Wear

Just like in standard Android apps, the list is one of the most important aspects of a user interface. In Wear the lists have changed to be easier to interact with while you're on the move.

You have two options when dealing with lists in Android Wear: WearableListView and GridView.

Using WearableListView

WearableListView is optimized for small screens. It scrolls vertically and has a snapping effect. To add WearableListView to your project, you need three things: the layout, the adapter, and the data. Let's start with the layout of the list (Listing 5-19).

LISTING 5-19: Creating the list row layout

```xml
<?xml version="1.0" encoding="utf-8"?>

<RelativeLayout
  xmlns:android="http://schemas.android.com/apk/res/android"
  xmlns:wear="http://schemas.android.com/apk/res-auto"
  android:orientation="vertical"
  android:layout_width="match_parent"
  android:layout_height="wrap_content">

  <android.support.wearable.view.CircledImageView
    android:layout_width="wrap_content"
    android:layout_height="wrap_content"
    android:id="@+id/row_image"
    android:src="@drawable/ic_launcher"
    wear:circle_radius="20dp"
    wear:circle_color="#00cc99"
    android:layout_centerVertical="true"
    android:layout_alignParentStart="true"/>
```

continues

LISTING 5-19: *(continued)*

```
    <TextView
      android:layout_width="wrap_content"
      android:layout_height="wrap_content"
      android:textAppearance="?android:attr/textAppearanceLarge"
      android:text="Large Text"
      android:id="@+id/row_text"
      android:layout_gravity="center_horizontal"
      android:layout_toEndOf="@+id/view"
      android:layout_centerVertical="true"
      android:layout_centerHorizontal="true"/>
</RelativeLayout>
```

The `WearableListView.Adapter` class is slightly different from what you're probably used to in standard Android. It's an abstract class, which means you need to create a subclass. It has three methods you need to work with: `onCreateViewHolder()`, `onBindViewHolder()`, and `getItemCount()`. Listing 5-20 shows a simple example of how to use them.

LISTING 5-20: Building the list adapter

```java
public class MyAdapter extends WearableListView.Adapter {

  Context mContext;
  LayoutInflater mLayoutInflater;
  String[] listData;

  public MyAdapter(Context context, String[] data) {
    mContext = context;
    mLayoutInflater = LayoutInflater.from(context);
    listData = data;
  }

  @Override
  public WearableListView.ViewHolder onCreateViewHolder(ViewGroup viewGroup,
                                                        int type) {
    return new WearableListView.ViewHolder(mLayoutInflater.inflate(R.layout
        .my_listitem, null));
  }

  @Override
  public void onBindViewHolder(WearableListView.ViewHolder viewHolder, int pos) {
    TextView text = (TextView) viewHolder.itemView.findViewById(R.id.row_text);
    text.setText(listData[pos]);
    viewHolder.itemView.setTag("item" + pos);
  }

  @Override
  public int getItemCount() {
    return listData.length;
  }
}
```

In Wear the adapter has become much simpler than it was in standard Android. For one thing, you don't need to build your own holders anymore—which is something I occasionally forget. In the method `onCreateViewHolder()` you simply inflate a layout for your row. The returning view is the `ViewHolder` for your list.

`onBindViewHolder()` is where you link your data to the respective UI widgets inside your layout file.

Finally, you return the length of your list data in the `getItemCount()` method. Where you store your data is up to you. In this example I chose to pass it as a reference to the constructor of the adapter.

When it's time to put your list to the test, all you need is three lines of code, as shown in Listing 5-21, the data (in this example a `String` array), the list, and the adapter.

LISTING 5-21: Putting it all together

```
String[] data = {"Item 1", "Item 2", "Item 3", "Item 4", "Item 5"};
WearableListView list = (WearableListView) findViewById(R.id.listview);
list.setAdapter(new MyAdapter(this, data));
```

Figure 5-14 shows the list in all its glory.

FIGURE 5-14: The list view with custom row layout

Of course, you also can add click actions to your `WearableListView`, just like you can with any other `View`. Use the special `ClickListener` interface located in the `WearableListView` class, as shown in Listing 5-22.

LISTING 5-22: Making the ClickListener class

```
private class MyListListener implements WearableListView.ClickListener {

    @Override
    public void onClick(WearableListView.ViewHolder viewHolder) {
      Toast.makeText(MyActivity.this, "Clicked on: " + viewHolder.itemView
          .getTag(), Toast.LENGTH_LONG).show();
    }
```

continues

LISTING 5-22: *(continued)*

```
    @Override
    public void onTopEmptyRegionClick() {
    }
  }
}
```

Then simply attach the listener to your list, as shown in Listing 5-23.

LISTING 5-23: Attaching a listener

```
String[] data = {"Item 1", "Item 2", "Item 3", "Item 4", "Item 5"};
WearableListView list = (WearableListView) findViewById(R.id.listview);
list.setAdapter(new MyAdapter(this, data));
list.setClickListener(new MyListListener());
```

As you've seen, WearableListView is very handy. It gives you a list that follows the general guidelines for Wear apps and is very easy to implement. You also have alternatives such as GridViewPager, also known as 2D Picker.

The 2D Picker

Much like the list, the grid consists of a layout, an adapter, and data. But the big difference is the data. In a normal list it's one-dimensional, but in grid view its two-dimensional—the user can scroll in both dimensions freely. This example uses CardFragment to quickly produce pages, but you can create your own page layout too.

Start by creating your adapter. It should inherit from the GridPagerAdapter class, as shown in Listing 5-24.

LISTING 5-24: Creating the grid adapter

```
public class MyGridAdapter extends FragmentGridPagerAdapter {

  String[][] mData;

  public MyGridAdapter(FragmentManager fm, String[][] data) {
    super(fm);
    mData = data;
  }

  @Override
  public Fragment getFragment(int row, int col) {
    CardFragment fragment = CardFragment.create("A page", "Page " + row + "," +
        "" + col);
    return fragment;
  }
```

```
    @Override
    public int getRowCount() {
      return mData.length;
    }

    @Override
    public int getColumnCount(int row) {
      return mData[row].length;
    }
  }
```

When the Adapter is ready, the next step is to add a `GridViewPager` to your layout, as shown in Listing 5-25.

LISTING 5-25: Building your app layout

```xml
<?xml version="1.0" encoding="utf-8"?>

<LinearLayout
  xmlns:android="http://schemas.android.com/apk/res/android"
  android:orientation="vertical"
  android:layout_width="match_parent"
  android:layout_height="match_parent">

  <android.support.wearable.view.GridViewPager
    android:layout_width="match_parent"
    android:layout_height="match_parent"
    android:id="@+id/grid"/>
</LinearLayout>
```

Finally, glue it all together in your activity, as shown in Listing 5-26.

LISTING 5-26: Composing the 2D Picker

```java
GridViewPager pager = (GridViewPager) findViewById(R.id.grid);
String[][] data = {
    {"Row 1, col 1", "Row 1, col 2", "Row 1, col 3"},
    {"Row 2, col 1", "Row 2, col 2", "Row 2, col 3"},
    {"Row 3, col 1", "Row 3, col 2", "Row 3, col 3"}};
pager.setAdapter(new MyGridAdapter(getFragmentManager(), data));
```

Your result should resemble Figure 5-15.

FIGURE 5-15: The 2D Picker

PROVIDING POSITIVE FEEDBACK

A key feature of Wear is feedback. It's critical that you give your users clear and timely feedback within the short period of time that you have their attention. Google provides three kinds of basic animation feedback that you can use as necessary. All of them are launched using the `ConfirmationActivity` class:

➤ The confirmation animation is a green check box that disappears by itself. It is often used to show that something was done for you on the phone, such as adding an event to a calendar or taking a note. The idea is that the user doesn't have to open the phone and verify that the item was added.

➤ Open-on-phone shows an animated check box that indicates that something was sent to the phone. It's a hint that the user should review the action on the phone.

➤ The action-failed animation—the sad cloud—stays onscreen until the user actively removes it and attempts to complete the action again.

To use `ConfirmationActivity`, you create a subclass and add it to your manifest. Then you start the activity with the correct parameters. You have beautiful animations that run smoothly on your users' Wear device. Listing 5-27 shows how to subclass `ConfirmationActivity`.

LISTING 5-27: Creating a subclass of ConfirmationActivity

```
public class MyConfirmations extends ConfirmationActivity {
}
```

Add your new activity to your AndroidManifest.xml file, as shown in Listing 5-28.

LISTING 5-28: Adding your confirmation activity to the manifest

```
<?xml version="1.0" encoding="utf-8"?>
<manifest xmlns:android="http://schemas.android.com/apk/res/android"
          package="com.wiley.wrox.chapter5">
  <uses-feature android:name="android.hardware.type.watch"/>
  <application
    android:allowBackup="true"
    android:icon=@drawable/ic_launcher"
    android:label=@string/app_name"
    android:theme=@android:style/Theme.DeviceDefault">
    ...
    <activity android:name=".MyConfirmations"/>
  </application>

</manifest>
```

After you have registered the class for your app, it must be started with the correct settings. Table 5-5 lists the extra information you need to pass with the intent.

TABLE 5-5: Extra information for ConfirmationActivity

FIELD	DESCRIPTION
EXTRA_ANIMATION_TYPE	The type of the animation. Can be either FAILURE_ANIMATION, OPEN_ON_PHONE_ANIMATION, or SUCCESS_ANIMATION.
EXTRA_MESSAGE	A short text message to display along with the animation.

Starting the Success Feedback

Listing 5-29 shows how to start the success animation.

LISTING 5-29: Starting the success confirmation

```
Intent success = new Intent(MyActivity.this, MyConfirmations.class);
success.putExtra(ConfirmationActivity.EXTRA_ANIMATION_TYPE,
    ConfirmationActivity.SUCCESS_ANIMATION);
success.putExtra(ConfirmationActivity.EXTRA_MESSAGE, "This is OK!");
startActivity(success);
```

Figure 5-16 shows the success animation in all its glory.

FIGURE 5-16: The success animation

Starting the Open-on-Phone Animation

Starting the open-on-phone animation is no different, as shown in Listing 5-30.

LISTING 5-30: Starting the open-on-phone animation

```
phone.putExtra(ConfirmationActivity.EXTRA_ANIMATION_TYPE,
    ConfirmationActivity.OPEN_ON_PHONE_ANIMATION);
phone.putExtra(ConfirmationActivity.EXTRA_MESSAGE, "Check your phone!");
startActivity(phone);
```

This animation is slightly different, as shown in Figure 5-17.

FIGURE 5-17: The open-on-phone animation

Starting the Failure Feedback

The failure feedback is almost identical to the other two; only the type is different. See Listing 5-31.

LISTING 5-31: Starting the failure animation

```
Intent fail = new Intent(this, MyConfirmations.class);
fail.putExtra(ConfirmationActivity.EXTRA_ANIMATION_TYPE,
    ConfirmationActivity.FAILURE_ANIMATION);
fail.putExtra(ConfirmationActivity.EXTRA_MESSAGE, "Not OK!");
startActivity(fail);
```

Your result should look like Figure 5-18. Note that the failure animation stays until the user clicks it away.

FIGURE 5-18: The failure animation

SUMMARY

This chapter has described the new UI widgets available in Android Wear. You learned how to build apps using some of these new classes.

This chapter also introduced design principles for very small screens and gave you some points to keep in mind when building apps with Android Wear.

The next chapter explores how to add connectivity to Android Wear apps.

RECOMMENDED READING

Creative Vision for Android Wear, https://developer.android.com/design/wear/creative-vision.html.
Design Principles for Wear, https://developer.android.com/design/wear/principles.html.
UI Patterns for Wear, https://developer.android.com/design/wear/patterns.html.

Voice Input

WROX.COM CODE DOWNLOADS FOR THIS CHAPTER

The code downloads for this chapter are found at www.wrox.com/go/androidwearables on the Download Code tab. The code is in the Chapter 6 download and the files are individually named according to the listing numbers noted throughout the chapter.

TALKING TO YOUR WRIST

> [...] the phone is like your brain; it's controlling your TV or driving your car [...]
>
> — JUSTIN KOH, ANDROID WEAR DEVELOPER, GOOGLE I/O 2014

Do you remember Dick Tracy, the comic-strip detective who had a two-way wrist radio he used to talk to his boss at the police station? It is as if Android Wear is trying to re-create that vision of the future from almost 70 years ago.

Thirty-six years later, David Hasselhoff, playing the character Michael Knight, talked to his intelligent car, KITT, using a wristwatch on which he would get voice-generated answers from the car. According to some fan sites, the watch Hasselhoff wore was a modification of a *Star Wars*-branded watch manufactured by Bradley for the U.S. (I recommend that you search for images of both characters and their watches. We could not include any due to copyright restrictions.)

Android Wear offers half the communication capabilities of Dick's and Michael's radio watches. You can dictate commands to your Wear device, but it has no sound-playing capabilities. None of the existing Wear-enabled devices currently has any speakers or sound output. This is a forthcoming feature and will make it possible to stream audio via Buetooth toward external speakers.

On the other hand, all of them can be commanded via voice in multiple ways. This chapter introduces different types of voice input. The code listings give you basic information on how to use the different types of voice input. Check the chapter downloads for full code examples.

TYPES OF VOICE INTERACTION

There are different types of voice interaction. You could give your smartwatch simple commands, and it could recognize a series of predefined commands by comparing the sound input to a table of existing recordings to provide you with immediate feedback.

Or the device could transfer the stream of audio, once digitized, to the smartphone or tablet it is connected to for the other device to operate a voice recognition algorithm. Sending the voice information to, for example, a cloud service for remote storage or treatment would fall into the same category. In essence it is the same case where the smartwatch sends the data to a different system for it to deal with it.

> **NOTE** *During the Google I/O conference in 2014, the lecture "Android Wear: The Developer's Perspective" covered topics concerning Android Wear. The audience posed several questions about the use of voice interaction.*
>
> *Watching that video at* `http://youtu.be/sha_w3_5c2c` *can help you understand some of the principles behind the use of voice commands. The Q&A session begins two-thirds of the way through the video.*

Finally, the smartwatch (or any other Wear-enabled device) could simply use voice interaction to react to a notification coming from the phone or tablet. This interaction pattern is slightly different, because the smartwatch pushes commands or data toward the device it's paired to. In this case, the phone expects an answer in textual form that will be entered via voice. The screen real estate isn't optimized for a virtual keyboard.

It's not that easy to conceptually understand these cases by reading Android's documentation site. Table 6-1 shows all the possibilities for the use of voice within Android Wear to help you choose the one you need for your project. In this chapter you'll get to try all of them.

Each interaction mode requires a different set of commands on the phone's Android application package (APK) and the Wear device's APK to get both programs to work in sync. The only exception is the last case—running commands without a connected device.

TABLE 6-1: Types of Voice Interaction

INTERACTION	DESCRIPTION
Send a command to the host	The Wear device computes a voice recognition operation and sends a command to the host device. In the official documentation, this is called *app-provided voice capabilities*.
Send a text to the host	The Wear device captures the audio and pushes it through its codec to produce a stream of bytes of audio that can be sent to the host device.
Respond to a query from the host	When a notification arrives, it is possible to get a set of predefined answers to which the user can simply answer using voice.
Respond to a query from the host in a text	When a notification arrives from, for example, an e-mail, it is possible to answer by talking into the Wear device and to get the speech transcribed into a text to send as an answer.
Execute simple system commands	The Wear device computes a voice recognition operation based on a series of predefined intents. In the official documentation, this is called *system-provided voice capabilities*.

> **NOTE** *Quoting Justin Koh, one of the Android Wear developers shown in the video mentioned earlier: "Voice is an array of bytes. Make sure you have the right codecs."*
>
> *In other words, if you plan to use your Wear device as a remote microphone, make sure the specific device you want your app to run on can encode and decode the digital audio in the right format.*
>
> *The codec compresses the raw audio data to make it lighter. At the other end, the device receiving the stream needs a compatible codec to decompress the audio.*
>
> *For an overview on the supported media formats within Android see* `https://developer.android.com/guide/appendix/media-formats.html`.

It is possible to enhance existing apps using voice input. Apps created prior to the launch of Wear cannot be used with voice commands unless they are remade to include the proper intents on the APK on the phone and the APK on the smartwatch. In other words, if you want your existing app to include voice interaction using Wear, you must do the following:

1. Add the proper intents on the phone's APK so that it can, for example, be ready to take text input via the watch's voice recognition system.

2. Create an APK for the watch that allows data entry via voice when requested.

The Wear SDK has been created to make this integration seamless. Adding voice input takes just a couple keystrokes. But remember that even if the technology allows you to, for example, make every text input field in your application Wear-enabled, you still need to ensure that the interaction pattern makes sense.

USING SYSTEM-PROVIDED VOICE COMMANDS

The Android Wear platform provides several voice intents that are based on simple user actions. Table 6-2 lists the actions you can use. When you use voice commands, all your sentences need to start with "OK, Google." This phrase is unique enough for the Wear device not to be triggered randomly.

TABLE 6-2: Predefined Voice Intents According to the Official Wear Documentation

NAME	SAMPLE PHRASES	INTENT (VALUES OF THE CONSTANT)		
		ACTION	CATEGORY/ MIME-TYPE	EXTRAS
Call a car/taxi	"OK, Google, get me a taxi." "OK, Google, call me a car."	`com.google. android.gms. actions.RESERVE_ TAXI_RESERVATION`		
Take a note	"OK, Google, take a note." "OK, Google, note to self."	`android.intent. action.SEND`	`com.google .android .voicesearch. SELF_NOTE`	`android.content .Intent.EXTRA_TEXT` A string with note body
Set alarm	"OK, Google, set an alarm for 8 a.m." "OK, Google, wake me up at 6 tomorrow."	`android.intent. action.SET_ALARM`		`android.provider .AlarmClock.EXTRA_HOUR` An integer with the hour of the alarm `android.provider .AlarmClock .EXTRA_MINUTES` An integer with the minute of the alarm (These two extras are optional. Either neither or both are provided.)
Set timer	"OK, Google, set a timer for 10 minutes."	`android.intent. action.SET_TIMER`		`android.provider .AlarmClock. EXTRA_LENGTH` An integer in the range of 1 to 86,400 (the number of seconds in 24 hours) representing the length of the timer

NAME	SAMPLE PHRASES	INTENT (VALUES OF THE CONSTANT)		
		ACTION	CATEGORY/ MIME-TYPE	EXTRAS
Start/ Stop a bike ride	"OK, Google, start cycling." "OK, Google, start my bike ride." "OK, Google, stop cycling."	`vnd.google. fitness.TRACK`	`vnd.google. fitness. activity/biking`	`actionStatus` A string with the value `ActiveActionStatus` when starting and `CompletedActionStatus` when stopping
Start/stop a run	"OK, Google, track my run." "OK, Google, start running." "OK, Google, stop running."	`vnd.google. fitness.TRACK`	`vnd.google. fitness. activity/running`	`actionStatus` A string with the value `ActiveActionStatus` when starting and `CompletedActionStatus` when stopping
Start/stop a workout	"OK, Google, start a workout." "OK, Google, track my workout." "OK, Google, stop workout."	`vnd.google. fitness.TRACK`	`vnd.google. fitness. activity/other`	`actionStatus` A string with the value `ActiveActionStatus` when starting and `CompletedActionStatus` when stopping
Show heart rate	"OK, Google, what's my heart rate?" "OK, Google, what's my bpm?"	`vnd.google. fitness.VIEW`	`vnd.google. fitness.data_ type/com.google. heart_rate.bpm`	
Show step count	"OK, Google, how many steps have I taken?" "OK, Google, what's my step count?"	`vnd.google. fitness.VIEW`	`vnd.google. fitness.data_ type/com.google. step_count. cumulative`	

ABOUT INTENTS

Intents allow you to launch an activity in another application by describing a simple action to be performed (such as "edit picture" or "view map") in an `Intent` object. This type of intent specifies an action and provides some data with which to perform it. It is therefore called implicit intent.

When calling `startActivity()` or `startActivityForResult()` as an implicit intent, the system resolves the intent to an application that can handle the intent and starts its corresponding activity. If more than one application could handle the intent, the system would present the user with a dialog from which to pick an app.

You can read more about intents at `http://developer.android.com/guide/components/intents-filters.html`.

Just Launch an App

Try the capabilities of your smartwatch. Note that you cannot do so by using an emulator connected to a phone over the USB. According to different reports, it is not possible to use voice commands from the emulator to trigger events on the phone. This will not work for either system-predefined commands or app-predefined ones.

NOTE *The current emulator does not support voice actions via the keyboard, even though the text appears on the display. This is the standard test procedure (using the keyboard to issue voice commands), because the emulator cannot use the microphone in your PC.*

Therefore, if you want to start an app you launched in your emulator, you must do the following:

1. *Click the display.*

2. *Click the red G.*

3. *Go to the Start menu and choose the app from there.*

You can also quickly start the application using something like this from your development machine:

```
adb shell am start -n com.example.android.test/.TestActivity
```

To launch an app, just talk to your Wear device. Say, "OK, Google, start HelloWorld." If you still have your first application installed on the device, it should launch.

Hack an Existing Intent to Launch Your App

As hinted earlier, when talking about intents, it is possible to "hijack" an existing intent to launch your own application. You just need to modify the AndroidManifest.xml file to your app so that it is listed as one of the possible actions to take upon the arrival of the intents defined in Table 6-2. Remember that it is possible to hack any intent within Android. Listing 6-1 shows the filter you need to add to the activity you want to launch in your manifest file to get it to be triggered with the call of a timer. For example, you could launch your HelloWorld app when telling your smartwatch "OK, Google, set a timer for 10 minutes."

LISTING 6-1: Intent filter to enable launching your app when setting a timer

```
<intent-filter>
  <action android:name="android.intent.action.SET_TIMER"/>
  <category android:name="android.intent.category.DEFAULT"/>
</intent-filter>
```

Launch Your App with Voice the "Right" Way

Besides trying to take over an existing intent in your smartwatch, you also can use a different way in your wearable's AndroidManifest.xml file to get the system to call your app when saying "OK, Google, start myApp." By default your app's android:name attribute to the activity tag is .MyActivity. (If you are looking at the downloadable example for this chapter, it is .MyActivityWearable.) As shown in Listing 6-2, just add a second activity called StartRunActivity with the proper intent filter, install the app on your watch, and it should work.

LISTING 6-2: Activity to enable launching your app via voice

```
<activity android:name="StartRunActivity" android:label="@string/app_name">
    <intent-filter>
        <action android:name="android.intent.action.MAIN" />
        <category android:name="android.intent.category.LAUNCHER" />
    </intent-filter>
</activity>
```

THE WEAR APIs

The wearable services within Wear consist of three APIs that help the application software on the phone or tablet easily communicate with the Wear device: the data API, the message API, and the node API. Each takes care of different parts of the information exchange between devices.

All can be called from both the phone app and the wearable one, and all your data can be used on both sides. WearableListenerService implements all the listeners for the different APIs.

Using voice as an input, in any of the forms explained in Table 6-1, requires the devices to communicate with each other. Therefore, understanding the role of each API is important at this point.

Data API

The data API lets you put data on a sort of virtual cache shared among the connected devices. You don't need to worry about anything but putting the data into storage and taking it from there at either side.

This is convenient when dealing with images, because you don't have to send them repeatedly, thus saving battery life.

Message API

The message API sends byte arrays between the devices. Suppose you are capturing voice on the watch and sending it, after it is digitized, to the phone. As long as you push your audio information as a byte array, you can get direct access to the message API and send the information directly.

Node API

The node API checks when nodes enter the connection range. This function can be used to discover whether the phone is present. After a while it should be straightforward to simply put the device to sleep if too much time has passed since the last connection was detected.

ANSWERING TO NOTIFICATIONS: CAPTURING YOUR VOICE INTO AN APP

In the following section you will write an example in which voice plays a big role. In this case you will start by creating a new project with apps for both a phone and a Wear device. Chapter 5 showed you how to create a new project from scratch involving both a mobile and a Wear device. This chapter gets you a little further. Its aim is getting you up and running with a hybrid development system using a phone and a Wear emulator that talk to each other.

It is possible to run almost any kind of scenario between emulators and real devices, knowing the limitations of launching applications or triggering intents. In these two examples you will experiment with a phone running Android's version of KitKat (which should work on any later version) and an emulator of a Wear smartwatch. In this way you can send events from one to the other.

> **NOTE** *Remember the basic usage of the emulator as soon as it is up and running and as soon as your phone is connected to your computer:*
>
> ➤ *You need to link the emulator with the phone using* adb. *The command to do so is* adb -s <phone_ID> forward tcp:5601 tcp:5601.
>
> ➤ *To get the phone's identification number, issue the command* adb devices *and copy the proper id from there.*
>
> *If you disconnect the phone or reboot the emulator, you need to reissue this command.*

Notifications including an action to input text, such as replying to an e-mail, should normally launch an activity on the Wear device to input the text. As mentioned earlier, Wear devices—currently smartwatches—have little space for displaying a keyboard, so you can let users dictate a reply or provide predefined text messages using RemoteInput.

In this first case you will make a wear and a phone app that communicate with each other. When launched, the phone application sends a request (in the form of a notification) for a voice answer on the Wear device.

This gets the Wear device to show a query for a voice answer onscreen. The user is prompted to talk to the device. The answer is captured by RemoteInput, and the wear application displays the result onscreen while it sends it back to the phone application. Finally, the phone application shows the result on a text field.

The following sections show how this simple application is made.

Creating a Simple App Sending a Notification

Chapter 4 explored the different types of notifications on a Wear device. This time you will use the simplest one, a button running on your phone's screen, to trigger an event on the smartwatch emulator.

Creating Your Empty Project

Follow these steps to create your new Android Wear project:

1. Click New Project in the Android Studio startup dialog or on the menu, and enter the correct information for your app, as shown in Figure 6-1. I'm calling my app SimpleNotification and placing it in the com.wiley.wrox.chapter6.simplenotification package. Click Next or press **Alt+N** to continue.

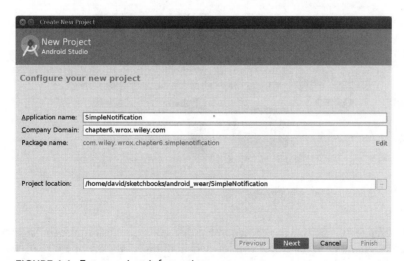

FIGURE 6-1: Enter project information

2. As shown in Figure 6-2, I selected Phone and Tablet API 19 to match the specific version of the Android OS on my phone. You should choose the one that matches your own phone. I also chose Wear API 20. Then click Next.

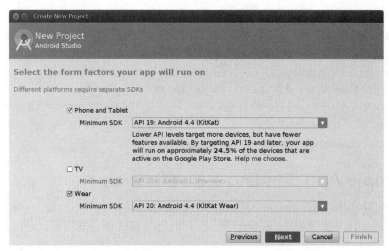

FIGURE 6-2: Select form factors and API levels for your app

3. Choose Blank Activity to add a blank activity to your mobile, as shown in Figure 6-3, and click Next twice to accept the default parameters.

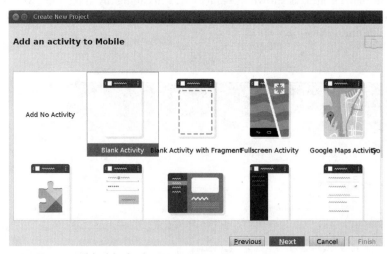

FIGURE 6-3: Add a blank phone activity

4. Choose a name for the activity, as shown in Figure 6-4. I chose not to use the default one this time to make it simpler in the editor window when multiple tabs are open. I call the activity **MyActivityPhone** and the layout **activity_my_phone**.

FIGURE 6-4: Choose a name for the activity

5. Choose Blank Wear Activity, as shown in Figure 6-5. By default this is a standard activity with `WatchViewStub` as the main layout file. Click Next.

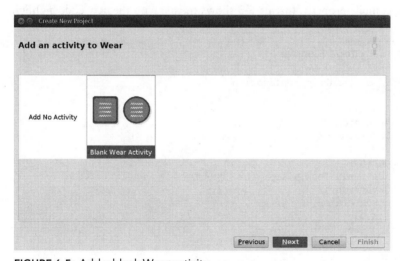

FIGURE 6-5: Add a blank Wear activity

6. Notice in Figure 6-6 that Android Studio creates two layouts, **round_activity_my_wear** and **rect_activity_my_wear**. For consistency, I named the activity **MyActivityWear** and the layout **activity_my_wear**. To create your new Mobile + Wear app, click Finish.

You should now have an Android Studio project that has two application structures within it called *mobile* and *wear*.

FIGURE 6-6: Edit the properties for your Wear activity and layouts

Modifying the Gradle File

The gradle file for the mobile app needs to include a reference to a series of dependencies needed for this app bundle to compile properly. Listing 6-3 shows the file with the new code highlighted.

LISTING 6-3: Adding dependencies

```
apply plugin: 'com.android.application'

android {
    compileSdkVersion 20
    buildToolsVersion "20.0.0"

    defaultConfig {
        applicationId "com.wiley.wrox.chapter6.simplenotification"
        minSdkVersion 19
        targetSdkVersion 20
        versionCode 1
        versionName "1.0"
    }
    buildTypes {
        release {
            runProguard false
            proguardFiles getDefaultProguardFile('proguard-android.txt'),
                'proguard-rules.pro'
        }
    }
}

dependencies {
    compile fileTree(dir: 'libs', include: ['*.jar'])
```

```
        wearApp project(':wear')
        compile 'com.google.android.gms:play-services-wearable:+'



        compile 'com.android.support:support-v4:20.0+'
}
```

Modifying the App's Layout

By default the app comes with a simple layout featuring the default icon for apps as well as the classic "Hello world!" message, as shown in Figure 6-7.

A good way to continue is to add a button to send notifications to the Wear device when pressed, as well as to add the classic Wrox logotype to the application. To implement this modification, you need to add some code to the activity_my_phone.xml definition file. Listing 6-4 highlights the changes I decided to implement in this case. I just added code to implement a button with the callback function simpleNotification. Figure 6-8 shows the result.

FIGURE 6-7: The default layout of the mobile app on the simulator

FIGURE 6-8: An app with an extra button on the simulator

LISTING 6-4: Changes on the layout from the original file

```
<RelativeLayout xmlns:android="http://schemas.android.com/apk/res/android"
    xmlns:tools="http://schemas.android.com/tools"
    android:layout_width="match_parent"
    android:layout_height="match_parent"
    android:paddingLeft="@dimen/activity_horizontal_margin"
    android:paddingRight="@dimen/activity_horizontal_margin"
    android:paddingTop="@dimen/activity_vertical_margin"
    android:paddingBottom="@dimen/activity_vertical_margin"
    tools:context=".MyActivityPhone">

    <TextView
        android:id="@+id/textView"
        android:text="@string/hello_world"
        android:layout_width="wrap_content"
        android:layout_height="wrap_content" />

    <Button
        style="?android:attr/buttonStyleSmall"
        android:layout_width="match_parent"
        android:layout_height="wrap_content"
        android:text="Simple Notification"
        android:id="@+id/button"
        android:onClick="simpleNotification"
        android:layout_below="@+id/textView"
        android:layout_centerHorizontal="true"
        android:layout_marginTop="22dp" />
</RelativeLayout>
```

To change the logotype, you need to add Wrox's logotype to the resources folder to a subfolder called **drawable-xxhdpi**. That will let you access it from within the AndroidManifest.xml file for your phone. Listing 6-5 shows the modifications on the default manifest file to include the new logotype as well as assign a launch mode.

> **NOTE** *There are four different ways to start an Android application (or launch mode). The* singleTop *option creates an application that will try to respond to the intents registered for it from the same instance of the activity, rather than making new instances of the same application in case it happens to be at the top of the activity stack. You can read more about this at* http://developer .android.com/guide/topics/manifest/activity-element.html.

LISTING 6-5: Changes to the original AndroidManifest.xml file

```
<?xml version="1.0" encoding="utf-8"?>
<manifest xmlns:android="http://schemas.android.com/apk/res/android"
    package="com.wiley.wrox.chapter6.simplenotification" >

    <application
        android:allowBackup="true"
```

```
android:icon="@drawable-xxhdpi/wrox_logo_big"
android:label="@string/app_name"
android:theme="@style/AppTheme" >
<activity
    android:name=".MyActivityPhone"
    android:label="@string/app_name"
    android:launchMode="singleTop" >
    <intent-filter>
        <action android:name="android.intent.action.MAIN" />
        <category android:name="android.intent.category.LAUNCHER" />
    </intent-filter>
</activity>
</application>

</manifest>
```

Figure 6-9 shows the app with the new image.

FIGURE 6-9: App with the Wrox logo

Adding the Right Callback Function

Adding the callback function is not a big deal in this case. Listing 6-6 highlights the additions you need to make to the default source code for it to run.

LISTING 6-6: Changes to the original MyActivityPhone.java file

```java
package com.wiley.wrox.chapter6.simplenotification;

import android.app.Activity;
import android.os.Bundle;
import android.view.Menu;
import android.view.MenuItem;
import android.app.Notification;
import android.support.v4.app.NotificationCompat;
import android.support.v4.app.NotificationManagerCompat;
import android.view.View;

public class MyActivityPhone extends Activity {

    private final static NOTIFICATION_ID = 6; // Use chapter number as ID
    private NotificationManagerCompat mNotificationManager;

    @Override
    protected void onCreate(Bundle savedInstanceState) {
        super.onCreate(savedInstanceState);
        setContentView(R.layout.activity_my_phone);

        mNotificationManager = NotificationManagerCompat.from(this);
    }

    @Override
    public boolean onCreateOptionsMenu(Menu menu) {
        // Inflate the menu; this adds items to the action bar if it is present.
        getMenuInflater().inflate(R.menu.my_activity_phone, menu);
        return true;
    }

    @Override
    public boolean onOptionsItemSelected(MenuItem item) {
        // Handle action bar item clicks here. The action bar will
        // automatically handle clicks on the Home/Up button, so long
        // as you specify a parent activity in AndroidManifest.xml.
        int id = item.getItemId();
        if (id == R.id.action_settings) {
            return true;
        }
        return super.onOptionsItemSelected(item);
    }
    public void simpleNotification(View v) {
        Notification notification = new NotificationCompat.Builder(this)
            .setSmallIcon(R.drawable.wrox_logo_small)
            .setContentTitle("My notification")
            .setContentText("My first wear notification!")
            .build();

        notif(notification);
```

```
    }

    private void notif(Notification n) {
        mNotificationManager.notify(NOTIFICATION_ID, n);
    }
}
```

After this code has been uploaded to a phone, when the button is clicked, the smartwatch simulator should capture the event with its default configuration. In other words, we haven't yet uploaded an app to the watch to do anything in conjunction with the handheld.

Figure 6-10 shows the notification to the watch on the simulator.

This SimpleNotification app is a good way to play around with the voice capabilities on the watch. It allows you to trigger voice input response requests when the notification is issued. This is very helpful for testing your new Wear-based apps.

FIGURE 6-10: Notification sent to the smartwatch simulator

Getting Your App to Receive a Voice Command

Given the previous SimpleNotification example, you will next build an application that requests an action from the user. The idea is that the answer is input via voice. Because the simulator has no voice input capabilities, you will use the keyboard to type your answers.

In this case, you will create an app for your handheld device that will be an improvement to the previous one. Below the button to send the notification, you will add a text box to capture the response from the user.

Figure 6-11 shows this new addition to the app.

When declaring the intent for the Wear device to issue its answer, you will use the `RemoteInput` class. This class tells the smartwatch to be ready to reply to the notification using voice as an input. The watch has everything that is needed for it to answer. In other words, you just need to make a phone app and not a Wear app in this case.

Revising the Callback Function

The callback function needs to include all the code related to the `RemoteInput` call. Listing 6-7 shows this new function added to the SimpleNotification app you worked with earlier. The new notification callback function is called `voiceNotification()`, which means I have removed the previous one.

FIGURE 6-11: Text field added to the UI

LISTING 6-7: Changes to the MyActivityPhone.java file

```java
package com.wiley.wrox.chapter6.simplenotification;
public class MyActivityPhone extends Activity {
    private final static NOTIFICATION_ID = 6; // Use chapter number as ID
    private NotificationManagerCompat mNotificationManager;

    public static final String EXTRA_MESSAGE = "extra_message";
    public static final String ACTION_DEMAND = "action_demand";
    public static final String EXTRA_VOICE_REPLY = "extra_voice_reply";

    @Override
    protected void onCreate(Bundle savedInstanceState) {
        super.onCreate(savedInstanceState);
        setContentView(R.layout.activity_my_phone);

        mNotificationManager = NotificationManagerCompat.from(this);
    }
[...]
    public void voiceNotification(View v) {

        Log.v("wrox", "Handheld sent notification");

        // Create the intent and pending intent for the notification
        Intent replyIntent = new Intent(this, DemandIntentReceiver.class)
                .putExtra(EXTRA_MESSAGE, "Reply selected.")
                .setAction(ACTION_DEMAND);
        PendingIntent replyPendingIntent =
            PendingIntent.getBroadcast(this.getApplicationContext(), 0,
            replyIntent, PendingIntent.FLAG_UPDATE_CURRENT);

        // Create the remote input
        String replyLabel = getResources().getString(R.string.reply_label);
        RemoteInput remoteInput = new RemoteInput.Builder(EXTRA_VOICE_REPLY)
            .setLabel(replyLabel)
            .build();

        // Create the reply action and add the remote input
        NotificationCompat.Action action =
            new NotificationCompat.Action.Builder(R.drawable.wrox_logo_small,
                getString(R.string.reply_label), replyPendingIntent)
                .addRemoteInput(remoteInput)
                .build();

        // Create the notification
        Notification replyNotification = new NotificationCompat.Builder(this)
            .setSmallIcon(android.R.drawable.ic_btn_speak_now)
            .setContentTitle("Voice to handheld")
            .setContentText("Left-swipe and do a voice reply")
            .extend(new NotificationCompat.WearableExtender().addAction(action))
            .build();

        // Issue the notification
        notif(replyNotification);
```

```
    }

    private void notif(Notification n) {
        mNotificationManager.notify(NOTIFICATION_ID, n);
    }
}
```

You will notice the three strings defined at the beginning of the class. Those are needed when creating the intent that we will use to capture the data coming back from the smartwatch. An intent has four parameters:

➤ The context of the activity: `this` in this case

➤ The class the intent refers to: `DemandIntentReceiver`

➤ Extra information to add details to the intent

➤ The type of action

Both the extra information and the type of action are user-defined. You need to define a string that will contain the value for those. This is how the broadcast receiver (which we will define next) can filter the data coming in.

Adding a Broadcast Receiver

We will capture the response from the Wear device by listening to a broadcast it will issue through the intent: `new Intent(this, DemandIntentReceiver.class)`. To do this, just add a new class to your project. In the first location you could just log the incoming data to logcat. In a later iteration of the code you could populate the text field on the app with the data coming from the smartwatch. This new class is shown in Listing 6-8.

LISTING 6-8: The new DemandIntentReceiver.java file

```
package com.wiley.wrox.chapter6.simplenotification;

import android.content.BroadcastReceiver;
import android.content.Context;
import android.content.Intent;
import android.os.Bundle;
import android.support.v4.app.RemoteInput;
import android.util.Log;

public class DemandIntentReceiver extends BroadcastReceiver {

    @Override
    public void onReceive(Context context, Intent intent) {
        Log.v("wrox", "got data");

        Bundle remoteInput = RemoteInput.getResultsFromIntent(intent);

        CharSequence reply =
```

continues

LISTING 6-8 *(continued)*

```
        remoteInput.getCharSequence(MyActivityPhone.EXTRA_VOICE_REPLY);
    if( reply != null){


        Log.v("wrox", "User reply from wearable: " + reply);
    }
  }
}
```

At this level, we are basically getting everything that comes to the broadcast receiver and just capturing EXTRA _ VOICE _ REPLY. It is possible to use the other filters defined in the app to separate the data from other broadcasts that are happening. However, doing so is not necessary at this point. Check the provided code examples for Chapter 6 to see yet another iteration of DemandIntentReceiver.java.

Modifying the App's Layout to Include a Text Field

To get the app ready to show the data received from the Wear device on the screen, you need to add a text field to the layout, as shown in Listing 6-9. You will also notice that here you need to change the name to the notification's callback function on the button's definition.

LISTING 6-9: Changes to activity_my_phone.xml

```xml
<RelativeLayout xmlns:android="http://schemas.android.com/apk/res/android"
    xmlns:tools="http://schemas.android.com/tools"
    android:layout_width="match_parent"
    android:layout_height="match_parent"
    android:paddingLeft="@dimen/activity_horizontal_margin"
    android:paddingRight="@dimen/activity_horizontal_margin"
    android:paddingTop="@dimen/activity_vertical_margin"
    android:paddingBottom="@dimen/activity_vertical_margin"
    tools:context=".MyActivityPhone">

    <TextView
        android:id="@+id/textView"
        android:text="@string/hello_world"
        android:layout_width="wrap_content"
        android:layout_height="wrap_content" />

    <Button
        style="?android:attr/buttonStyleSmall"
        android:layout_width="match_parent"
        android:layout_height="wrap_content"
        android:text="Simple Notification"
        android:id="@+id/button"
        android:onClick="voiceNotification"
        android:layout_below="@+id/textView"
        android:layout_centerHorizontal="true"
```

```
        android:layout_marginTop="22dp" />

<EditText
    android:layout_width="wrap_content"
    android:layout_height="wrap_content"
    android:id="@+id/reply_text"
    android:layout_below="@+id/button"
    android:layout_marginTop="22dp"
    android:layout_alignParentStart="true"
    android:layout_alignEnd="@+id/button"
    android:text="answer" />

</RelativeLayout>
```

Adding the New Class to the Manifest File

The new class has to be added to the manifest file within a receiver tag so that the program launches the receiver the way it should. Listing 6-10 shows the additions to the manifest file.

> **NOTE** *When adding components to your code through Android Studio's UI, the entries to the manifest file will be done automatically. A good reading introducing this feature, as well as some of the other advantages behind Android Studio, can be found at:* `http://www.airpair.com/android/android-studio-vs-eclipse.`

LISTING 6-10: Changes to the phone's AndroidManifest.xml

```
<?xml version="1.0" encoding="utf-8"?>
<manifest xmlns:android="http://schemas.android.com/apk/res/android"
    package="com.wiley.wrox.chapter6.simplenotification" >

    <application
        android:allowBackup="true"
        android:icon="@drawable-xxhdpi/wrox_logo_big"
        android:label="@string/app_name"
        android:theme="@style/AppTheme" >
        <activity
            android:name=".MyActivityPhone"
            android:label="@string/app_name"
            android:launchMode="singleTop" >
            <intent-filter>
                <action android:name="android.intent.action.MAIN" />

                <category android:name="android.intent.category.LAUNCHER" />
            </intent-filter>
```

continues

LISTING 6-10 *(continued)*

```
    </activity>

    <receiver android:name=".DemandIntentReceiver" android:exported="false">
        <intent-filter>
            <action android:name=
                "com.wiley.wrox.chapter6.simplenotification.ACTION_DEMAND"/>
        </intent-filter>
    </receiver>

</application>

<meta-data android:name="com.google.android.gms.version" android:value=
    "@integer/google_play_services_version" />

</manifest>
```

Adding the Reply String to the Strings File

We have added a new text field to the app. This requires a label. The name should be added as part of the strings.xml file in the resources folder. Listing 6-11 shows the new addition.

LISTING 6-11: Modification to strings.xml

```
<?xml version="1.0" encoding="utf-8"?>
<resources>

    <string name="app_name">SimpleNotification</string>
    <string name="hello_world">Hello world!</string>
    <string name="action_settings">Settings</string>
    <string name="reply_label">Voice reply</string>

</resources>
```

How It Works

Launch the app on your phone in parallel to the simulator. When you click the phone's notification button, the simulator shows the actual notification inviting you to swipe to the left and reply via voice, as shown in Figure 6-12.

After you swipe, you get a button you can use to reply to the notification, as shown in Figure 6-13.

If you click that icon, the voice input screen appears for you to type in your voice command. Figure 6-14 shows the input screen on the Wear device. Just type something (I assume you are using the emulator, just like I did, and therefore need to type first) and press Enter.

FIGURE 6-12:
Wear notification inviting you to enter a voice reply

FIGURE 6-13:
Reply button

FIGURE 6-14:
Reply button

FIGURE 6-15:
Wear device
sending back
data

Figure 6-15 shows the screen after you enter the data.

The broadcast receiver does the rest by showing the information you entered on the logcat. If you filter the incoming data with "wrox" as a filter, you should see the following three lines (to simplify, I took out the timestamps):

```
16199/com.wiley.wrox.chapter6.simplenotification V/wrox: Handheld sent notification

16199/com.[…].simplenotification V/wrox: got data

16199/com.[…].simplenotification V/wrox: User reply from wearable: hola
```

Showing the Answer on the App's Screen

Finally, you want to show the data you got from the Wear device on the app's screen. This is done by adding a `LocalBroadcastManager` to the main activity. Broadcast receivers exist for short periods of time (they are automatically killed by the operating system after a few seconds), therefore it is not possible to modify the UI on the main activity from them. The technique I recommend using to inform the UI of the arrival of data from the wearable is to add another receiver in the main activity and register it for an intent that will be produced by the `DemandIntentReceiver` class after getting valid data from the smartwatch. This implies making a couple of changes to both the `DemandIntentReceiver.java` file, but also to the `MyActivityPhone.java` file. Listing 6-12 shows how to improve the broadcast receiver to add the received text to the field on the app.

LISTING 6-12: Modification to DemandIntentReceiver.java

```java
@Override
public void onReceive(Context context, Intent intent) {
    Log.v("wrox", "got data");

    Bundle remoteInput = RemoteInput.getResultsFromIntent(intent);

    if (remoteInput.getCharSequence(
            MyActivityPhone.EXTRA_VOICE_REPLY) != null) {
        CharSequence reply =
            remoteInput.getCharSequence(MyActivityPhone.EXTRA_VOICE_REPLY);

        Log.v("wrox", "User reply from wearable: " + reply);

        Intent localIntent = new Intent("simplenotification.localIntent");
        localIntent.putExtra("result", reply.toString());
```

continues

LISTING 6-12 *(continued)*

```
        LocalBroadcastManager.getInstance(context)
            .sendBroadcast(localIntent);
    }
}
```

Listing 6-13 includes the additions to make to MyActivityPhone.java for it to register a
LocalBroadcastReceiver handler and capture the intents carrying the information coming from the
wearable after being proxied by the other Broadcast. This operation might seem redundant, it is possible to
make an inner class to the main activity capable of receiving the broadcasts from the wearable. However,
this way allows you to easily get the code to grow in the form of new classes contained in external files.

LISTING 6-13: Modifications to MyActivityPhone.java

```
BroadcastReceiver mResultReceiver;
  [...]
@Override
protected void onCreate(Bundle savedInstanceState) {
    super.onCreate(savedInstanceState);
    setContentView(R.layout.activity_my_phone);

    mResultReceiver = createBroadcastReceiver();
    LocalBroadcastManager.getInstance(this).registerReceiver(
        mResultReceiver,
        new IntentFilter("simplenotification.localIntent"));

    mNotificationManager = NotificationManagerCompat.from(this);
}
[...]
private void updateTextField(String text) {
    ((TextView)findViewById(R.id.reply_text)).setText(text);
}

private void notif(Notification n) {
    mNotificationManager.notify(NOTIFICATION_ID, n);
}

@Override
protected void onDestroy() {
    if (mResultReceiver != null) {
        LocalBroadcastManager.getInstance(this)
            .unregisterReceiver(mResultReceiver);
    }
    super.onDestroy();
}

private BroadcastReceiver createBroadcastReceiver() {
    return new BroadcastReceiver() {
```

```
        @Override
        public void onReceive(Context context, Intent intent) {
            updateTextField(intent.getStringExtra("result"));
        }
    };
}
```

Figure 6-16 shows the app on the phone after the data is retrieved and displayed on the designated text field.

FIGURE 6-16: Phone app showing the text

SUMMARY

This chapter was an overview of the power of using voice as an input to Wear devices. You can use different types of voice inputs. This chapter used "free speech" input, where you talk to your smartwatch as an answer to a notification sent from the phone.

You went through a step-by-step example to see how you can build your own voice-based apps starting from a default project created by Android Studio.

You also saw how to launch your existing apps using the voice command "OK, Google, *YourAppName.*"

There is a lot more you can do with voice. I recommend you take a look at the suggested readings as a way to continue your exploration.

In the next chapter you'll see how to extend the basic voice example created in this chapter to send your commands to the net and back.

RECOMMENDED READING

Read more about voice inputs as notifications, on the official Android documentation at `https://developer.android.com/training/wearables/notifications/voice-input.html`.

Pushing Data

WROX.COM CODE DOWNLOADS FOR THIS CHAPTER

The code downloads for this chapter are found at www.wrox.com/go/androidwearables on the Download Code tab. The code is in the Chapter 7 download and the filenames are those noted throughout the chapter.

Chapter 6 introduced the three APIs that handle all communication between your phone and your Wear device. This chapter is devoted to the Wearable Data Layer API. This set of methods and classes is part of Google Play services.

The API consists of a set of data objects and listeners that notify your apps of different events. Table 7-1 lists the available data objects.

TABLE 7-1: Data Objects in the Data API

OBJECT	DESCRIPTION
DataItem	Sets up shared data storage between the devices with automatic syncing.
MessageApi	Sends fire-and-forget-type commands, such as controlling and starting an intent on the wearable from the handheld or controlling a phone app from the wearable. Delivers an error when the devices are disconnected or the message if they are connected.
Asset	Sends binary blobs of data, such as images. Attached to data items, the system handles the transfer automatically. Minimizes Bluetooth bandwidth by caching large assets to avoid retransmission.
WearableListenerService	Used with services. Listens to data layer events.
DataListener	Used with foreground services. Listens to data layer events when the activity is in the foreground.

> **NOTE** *These APIs are specially designed for communication between handhelds and wearables. These are the APIs you should use to set up communication channels for your devices to talk to each other. Other methods, such as opening low-level sockets, should not be used at all for Wear devices.*

In this chapter you will experiment with different types of data transfers between devices. Doing so requires building a client to access the Google Play services. This client will provide a common entry point to all the services and will manage the network connection between the user's device and each Google service.

CHECKING THE EXAMPLE

Start by taking a look at the example that comes with the Android SDK 20 called DataLayer. Most likely, this example will be replicated in later releases of the SDK, so you should have a version of it available no matter which version of the Wear-enabled SDK you're using. It shows how different types of data can be moved back and forth between devices.

This example lets you take a picture with your phone's camera and send the picture to the smartwatch. Figure 7-1 explains how this works in the form of a diagram.

I have refactored the example so that it is made in the same way as the examples in the rest of the book. In the Chapter 7 code downloads folder, decompress the file named chapter7 _ SimpleWearableData.zip and open it in Android Studio. Once you have it running on your handheld and either your emulator or your watch, you can take a picture with your phone and send it to the Wear device's screen. You will also see a lot of information overlaid on top. Figure 7-2 shows the app running on a phone.

1. open communication line

2. take a picture with your phone

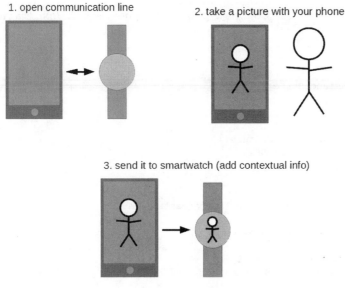

3. send it to smartwatch (add contextual info)

FIGURE 7-1: Diagram of the data transmission example

FIGURE 7-2: The Data transmission app on a phone

The interaction performed was to take a picture with the phone after pressing the button on the app's UI and then to send it to the wearable device. Unlike other examples, such as those in Chapter 6, in this case we have a running wearable app that waits to receive data from the phone and then displays it onscreen. Figure 7-3 is the result on an emulator for a squared Wear device.

The Wearable Data Layer API is useful when a chunk of information (such as an image or sound) needs to be transferred from one device to another. You need to make your own app for your smartwatch, because the amount of data to be transferred starts to become significant. Notifications aren't good for this. They offer a basic way to get simple information from one device to another and to gather an answer to a simple query. The default software on your Android Wear device won't meet all your needs—or will it?

FIGURE 7-3: The Data transmission app on a wearable

Since the whole codebase for this app is fairly large, we'll look at some code snippets from this example to understand how it works. Later you will perform the inverse operation of building such a program from scratch, which will help you better understand the minimal setup needed to make a distributed application between your Wear device and your phone or tablet.

Phone's MyActivityPhone.java

In this class you find a series of hints on what the application does. I have chosen a couple of code snippets and highlighted the most relevant aspects. Listing 7-1 shows that we are choosing to use the camera in the application and that when the class is created, the app builds a Google API client.

LISTING 7-1: Main Activity's onCreate method for the phone (filename: /mobile/src/main/java/.../MyActivityPhone.java)

```
@Override
public void onCreate(Bundle savedInstanceState) {
    super.onCreate(savedInstanceState);
    mHandler = new Handler();
    LOGD(TAG, "onCreate");
    mCameraSupported =
        getPackageManager().hasSystemFeature(
            PackageManager.FEATURE_CAMERA);
    setContentView(R.layout.activity_my_phone);
    setupViews();

    // Stores DataItems received by the local broadcaster
    // from the paired watch.
    mDataItemListAdapter = new DataItemAdapter(this,

        android.R.layout.simple_list_item_1);
    mDataItemList.setAdapter(mDataItemListAdapter);

    mGeneratorExecutor = new ScheduledThreadPoolExecutor(1);

    mGoogleApiClient = new GoogleApiClient.Builder(this)
        .addApi(Wearable.API)
        .addConnectionCallbacks(this)
        .addOnConnectionFailedListener(this)
        .build();
}
```

That Google API client implements listeners for all three APIs that are involved in the communication between devices: Data, Message, and Node. Listing 7-2 shows the override method that adds the listeners for all three APIs at once.

LISTING 7-2: Main Activity's onConnected method for the phone (filename: /mobile/src/main/java/.../MyActivityPhone.java) onConnected())

```
@Override //ConnectionCallbacks
public void onConnected(Bundle connectionHint) {
    LOGD(TAG, "Google API Client was connected");
    mResolvingError = false;
    mStartActivityBtn.setEnabled(true);
    mSendPhotoBtn.setEnabled(mCameraSupported);
    Wearable.DataApi.addListener(mGoogleApiClient, this);
    Wearable.MessageApi.addListener(mGoogleApiClient, this);
    Wearable.NodeApi.addListener(mGoogleApiClient, this);
}
```

The application, as mentioned earlier, takes a picture with the camera. It calls whatever camera applications you have installed, lets you choose one, and "intercepts" the result of that operation to include it in your app. It takes only a thumbnail, because the biggest image you can show on your Wear device is 320 by 320 pixels. Listing 7-3 shows the main methods responsible for this action. I have highlighted the lines that better describe this idea of launching the activity of taking a picture, resizing it, and sending it to the watch.

LISTING 7-3: Actions related to sending a picture to the wearable (filename: `/mobile/src/main/java/. . ./MyActivityPhone.java`)

```java
/**
 * Dispatches an {@link android.content.Intent} to take a photo. Result
 * will be returned in onActivityResult().
 */
private void dispatchTakePictureIntent() {
    Intent takePictureIntent = new Intent(MediaStore.ACTION_IMAGE_CAPTURE);
    if (takePictureIntent.resolveActivity(getPackageManager()) != null) {
        startActivityForResult(takePictureIntent, REQUEST_IMAGE_CAPTURE);
    }
}
/**
 * Builds an {@link com.google.android.gms.wearable.Asset} from a bitmap.
 * The image that we get back from the camera in "data" is a thumbnail
 * size. Typically, your image should not exceed 320x320, and if you want
 * to have zoom and parallax effect in your app, limit the size of your
 * image to 640x400. Resize your image before transferring to your

 * wearable device.

 */
private static Asset toAsset(Bitmap bitmap) {
    ByteArrayOutputStream byteStream = null;
    try {
        byteStream = new ByteArrayOutputStream();
        bitmap.compress(Bitmap.CompressFormat.PNG, 100, byteStream);
        return Asset.createFromBytes(byteStream.toByteArray());
    } finally {
        if (null != byteStream) {
            try {
                byteStream.close();
            } catch (IOException e) {
                // ignore
            }
        }
    }
}

/**
 * Sends the asset that was created from the photo we took by adding it

 * to the Data Item store.
 */
private void sendPhoto(Asset asset) {
    PutDataMapRequest dataMap = PutDataMapRequest.create(IMAGE_PATH);
    dataMap.getDataMap().putAsset(IMAGE_KEY, asset);
    dataMap.getDataMap().putLong("time", new Date().getTime());
```

continues

LISTING 7-3: *(continued)*

```java
        PutDataRequest request = dataMap.asPutDataRequest();
        Wearable.DataApi.putDataItem(mGoogleApiClient, request)
            .setResultCallback(new ResultCallback<DataItemResult>() {
                @Override
                public void onResult(DataItemResult dataItemResult) {
                    LOGD(TAG, "Sending image was successful: " +
                        dataItemResult.getStatus().isSuccess());
                }
            });

    }

    public void onTakePhotoClick(View view) {
        dispatchTakePictureIntent();
    }

    public void onSendPhotoClick(View view) {
        if (null != mImageBitmap && mGoogleApiClient.isConnected()) {
            sendPhoto(toAsset(mImageBitmap));
        }
    }
```

Even if the Node API is not the main aim of this chapter, it is worth showing the methods that deal with the connection between the smartwatch and the handheld. Thanks to this API, it's easy to look for existing wearables and send remote requests to start the activity. Listing 7-4 displays the methods and asynchronous class that check whether the watch is connected and fire up the activity remotely.

LISTING 7-4: Use of the Node API to fire the activity on the phone (filename: MainActivityPhone.java)

```java
    private Collection<String> getNodes() {
        HashSet<String> results = new HashSet<String>();
        NodeApi.GetConnectedNodesResult nodes =
            Wearable.NodeApi.getConnectedNodes(mGoogleApiClient).await();

        for (Node node : nodes.getNodes()) {
            results.add(node.getId());
        }

        return results;
    }

    private void sendStartActivityMessage(String node) {
        Wearable.MessageApi.sendMessage(
            mGoogleApiClient, node, START_ACTIVITY_PATH,

                new byte[0]).setResultCallback(
                    new ResultCallback<SendMessageResult>() {
```

```
                    @Override
                    public void onResult(SendMessageResult sendMessageResult) {
                        if (!sendMessageResult.getStatus().isSuccess()) {
                            Log.e(TAG, "Failed to send msg with status code: "
                            + sendMessageResult.getStatus().getStatusCode());
                        }
                    }
                }
            }
        );
}

private class StartWearableActivityTask extends AsyncTask<Void, Void, Void> {

    @Override
    protected Void doInBackground(Void... args) {
        Collection<String> nodes = getNodes();
        for (String node : nodes) {
            sendStartActivityMessage(node);
        }
        return null;
    }
}

/** Sends an RPC to start a fullscreen Activity on the wearable. */
public void onStartWearableActivityClick(View view) {
    LOGD(TAG, "Generating RPC");

    // Trigger an AsyncTask that will query for a list of connected
    // nodes and send a "start-activity" message to each connected node.
    new StartWearableActivityTask().execute();
}
```

Phone's AndroidManifest.xml

Note the following in the phone's manifest file which is shown in Listing 7-5.

➤ A uses-feature tag that specifies the use of the camera

➤ A meta-data tag that registers a key-value pair regarding the use of the Google Play services API

LISTING 7-5: Phone's manifest file (filename: /mobile/src/main/AndroidManifest.xml)

```
<?xml version="1.0" encoding="utf-8"?>
<manifest xmlns:android="http://schemas.android.com/apk/res/android"
    package="com.wiley.wrox.chapter7.simplewearabledata" >

    <uses-feature android:name=
        "android.hardware.camera" android:required="false" />

    <application
        android:allowBackup="true"
        android:icon="@drawable/ic_launcher"
```

continues

LISTING 7-5: *(continued)*

```
        android:label="@string/app_name"
        android:theme="@style/AppTheme" >

    <meta-data
        android:name="com.google.android.gms.version"
        android:value="@integer/google_play_services_version" />

    <activity
        android:name=".MyActivityPhone"
        android:label="@string/app_name"
        android:launchMode="singleTask" >
        <intent-filter>
            <action android:name="android.intent.action.MAIN" />

            <category android:name="android.intent.category.LAUNCHER" />
        </intent-filter>
    </activity>
</application>

</manifest>
```

> **NOTE** *As explained at* `http://developer.android.com/guide/topics/media/camera.html#manifest`, *you don't need to declare the use of the camera in the manifest file for your app using a* `uses-permission` *tag. The application itself isn't using the camera, but is launching an intent for a different app to capture a picture.*
>
> *At the same time, since the app will use the camera, but not as a hard requirement (if the camera is unavailable, that should not stop the app from working), the* `uses-feature` *tag is needed, with the specific value of* `android:required="false"`.
>
> *Sometimes you need to set up some app configuration information that has to be available across multiple classes. One example is storing API keys, version numbers, and so on. One way to store this information is by using the* `meta-data` *node within the AndroidManifest.xml file.*
>
> *This field can be used to store data of multiple types, like booleans, floats, ints, or strings. It can be accessed from your code using the* `Bundle` *method for your data type.*

Wearable's MyActivityWear.java

You will notice, when reading the Android Wear application in depth, that the program structure is very similar to the one for the handheld. A whole series of methods handle communication between both devices, initializing the three APIs, and so on.

In essence, the application on the smartwatch does three things:

➤ It shows a simple text when the phone's app hasn't been launched yet and/or the devices aren't connected to each other.

➤ When the phone captures a new image and sends it to the wearable, the application shows this image as a background picture.

➤ The application displays a series of status messages over the image. These messages come from the Node API or the Message API.

Listing 7-6 is an excerpt of the whole class. It focuses on the code that handles the arrival of the asset—the image in this case—the code that handles the shared data storage, and the code that handles how the wearable app displays it onscreen.

LISTING 7-6: Wearable application (filename: /wear/src/main/java/. . ./MyActivityWear.java)

```java
@Override
public void onDataChanged(DataEventBuffer dataEvents) {
    Log.d(TAG, "onDataChanged(): " + dataEvents);

    final List<DataEvent> events = FreezableUtils.freezeIterable(dataEvents);
    dataEvents.close();
    for (DataEvent event : events) {
        if (event.getType() == DataEvent.TYPE_CHANGED) {
            String path = event.getDataItem().getUri().getPath();
            if (DataLayerListenerService.IMAGE_PATH.equals(path)) {
                DataMapItem dataMapItem =

                    DataMapItem.fromDataItem(event.getDataItem());
                Asset photo = dataMapItem.getDataMap()
                    .getAsset(DataLayerListenerService.IMAGE_KEY);
                final Bitmap bitmap =

                    loadBitmapFromAsset(mGoogleApiClient, photo);
                mHandler.post(new Runnable() {
                    @Override
                    public void run() {
                        Log.d(TAG, "Setting background image..");
                        mLayout.setBackground(new BitmapDrawable(getResources(),

                            bitmap));
                    }
                });

            } else if (DataLayerListenerService.COUNT_PATH.equals(path)) {
                Log.d(TAG, "Data Changed for COUNT_PATH");
                generateEvent("DataItem Changed",

                    event.getDataItem().toString());
            } else {
```

continues

```
                    Log.d(TAG, "Unrecognized path: " + path);
                }

            } else if (event.getType() == DataEvent.TYPE_DELETED) {
                generateEvent("DataItem Deleted", event.getDataItem().toString());
            } else {
                generateEvent("Unknown data event type",

                    "Type = " + event.getType());
            }
        }
    }
    /**
     * Extracts {@link android.graphics.Bitmap} data from the
     * {@link com.google.android.gms.wearable.Asset}
     */
    private Bitmap loadBitmapFromAsset(GoogleApiClient apiClient, Asset asset) {
        if (asset == null) {
            throw new IllegalArgumentException("Asset must be non-null");
        }

        InputStream assetInputStream = Wearable.DataApi.getFdForAsset(
            apiClient, asset).await().getInputStream();

        if (assetInputStream == null) {
            Log.w(TAG, "Requested an unknown Asset.");
            return null;
        }
        return BitmapFactory.decodeStream(assetInputStream);
    }
```

Wearable's AndroidManifest.xml

The manifest file for the wearable contains a couple of relevant things, as shown in Listing 7-7. First, you see how the Google Play services API has been declared in the same way as in the manifest file for the phone's app.

Second, a class is launched as a service in parallel to the main class. This class, called `DataLayerListenerService`, waits for events coming from the handheld. There is a better description of that class in the following section.

Finally, the `intent-filter` named `com.wiley.wrox.chapter7.simplewearabledata.EXAMPLE` launches the app remotely.

```
[…]
<meta-data
    android:name="com.google.android.gms.version"
    android:value="@integer/google_play_services_version" />
```

```
<service
    android:name=".DataLayerListenerService" >
    <intent-filter>
        <action android:name="com.google.android.gms.wearable.BIND_LISTENER" />
    </intent-filter>
</service>


<activity
    android:name=".MyActivityWear"
    android:label="@string/app_name" >
    <intent-filter>
        <action android:name="android.intent.action.MAIN" />
        <category android:name="android.intent.category.LAUNCHER" />
    </intent-filter>
    <intent-filter>
        <action android:name=
            "com.wiley.wrox.chapter7.simplewearabledata.EXAMPLE"/>
        <category android:name="android.intent.category.DEFAULT"/>
    </intent-filter>
</activity>
[…]
```

Wearable's Listener

This example separates the wearable code into two classes—for clarity and because they perform two different tasks. The main activity changes the UI upon arrival of new background images or data that is worth pushing to the screen. The DataLayerListenerService is just that—a service running in the background that waits for events coming from the handheld app that it can report to the main class.

Listing 7-8 shows the two main methods in the service: onDataChanged and onMessageReceived. Note that the second one can launch the main class, as highlighted in the code.

LISTING 7-8: Wearable's listener class (filename: /wear/src/main/java/. . ./ DataLayerListenerService.java)

```
@Override
public void onDataChanged(DataEventBuffer dataEvents) {
    LOGD(TAG, "onDataChanged: " + dataEvents);
    final List<DataEvent> events = FreezableUtils.freezeIterable(dataEvents);
    dataEvents.close();
    if(!mGoogleApiClient.isConnected()) {
        ConnectionResult connectionResult = mGoogleApiClient
            .blockingConnect(30, TimeUnit.SECONDS);
        if (!connectionResult.isSuccess()) {
            Log.e(TAG, "DataLayerListenerService failed to connect to
```

continues

LISTING 7-8: *(continued)*

```
                    GoogleApiClient.");
              return;
          }
      }

      // Loop through the events and send a message back to the node
      // that created the data item.
      for (DataEvent event : events) {
          Uri uri = event.getDataItem().getUri();
          String path = uri.getPath();
          if (COUNT_PATH.equals(path)) {
              // Get the node id of the node that created the data item
              // from the host portion of the uri.
              String nodeId = uri.getHost();
              // Set the data of the message to be the bytes of the Uri.
              byte[] payload = uri.toString().getBytes();

              // Send the rpc
              Wearable.MessageApi.sendMessage(mGoogleApiClient, nodeId,

                  DATA_ITEM_RECEIVED_PATH, payload);
          }
      }
  }

  @Override
  public void onMessageReceived(MessageEvent messageEvent) {
      LOGD(TAG, "onMessageReceived: " + messageEvent);

      // Check to see if the message is to start an activity
      if (messageEvent.getPath().equals(START_ACTIVITY_PATH)) {
          Intent startIntent = new Intent(this, MyActivityWear.class);
          startIntent.addFlags(Intent.FLAG_ACTIVITY_NEW_TASK);
          startActivity(startIntent);
      }
  }
```

MAKING YOUR GOOGLE API CLIENT FROM SCRATCH

After you have checked the basic example from the Android Wear developers on how to get the phone app and the one on the watch to talk to each other, you will wonder how to make this from scratch. Let's build the scaffolding for a minimal application that you could expand for whatever use you're interested in.

A good implementation of a client to Google's API should be able to connect to one or more Google Play services synchronously or asynchronously and handle connection failures.

Next you will build two apps that will be connected through Google Play services. You will do the equivalent of having two sockets open between the phone and the watch. One will send a value to change the color of the watch's screen. The other will tell the handheld about the coordinates of the last touch on the watch's screen.

Consider the following points when dealing with such a scenario:

➤ **How will you handle communication between devices?** In this case we are using the Data API. You might consider it not to be optimal in this situation. Because we will send small amounts of data, the Message API probably would have been more suitable for this example. But because the aim is to show an example that is easy to expand, the Data API is more versatile and therefore is the one I chose.

➤ **How will you update the information on the devices' screens?** This was covered in Chapter 6, where we used `BroadcastReceiver` to listen to the arrival of digitized voice from the watch and a `LocalBroadcastManager` to capture the data into the UI. This time you will apply that same technique to the wearable and not only to the phone.

When it comes to the code's structure, you will have two classes for each device. One will be dedicated to the UI, and the other will run as a service, to listen to the changes in the data storage. When a change occurs, the service on the phone will tell the UI which new values it can use. The process will be the same for the wearable.

Start with a Clean Project

The first step is to create the API client by starting from a clean Android Wear project with code for both the handheld and the Wear device. In this case, a couple objects of the class `DataItem` are shared between both devices. One field represents the watch's background color, and the other represents the coordinates of the last location where the user touched the screen.

This is probably one of the shortest examples you can find on how to establish bidirectional communication between the handheld and the watch. It has many anchor points where you can easily add your own code.

The following sections examine each program that is part of this example. The code files can be downloaded from the Chapter 7 download folder.

The Phone's MyActivityPhone.java

On MyActivityPhone.java, as I have uploaded it to the Wrox server, you will find some interesting things:

➤ The declaration of a Google API client to start sharing data between devices, with overrides to control the possibility of the connectivity's being lost or not even started.

➤ A local broadcast manager that will be registered at the `onCreate()` method. It refreshes the text on the UI's label upon data arrival.

➤ The method `syncDataItem()`, which sends a new random color using the filter `PHONE2WEAR` to the watch every time someone presses the button on the UI. I used two different types of data within the Data API: an `int` for the color and a `String` to send a simple text indicating how many times the button has been pressed.

Listing 7-9 shows how to implement the Google API client from scratch.

LISTING 7-9: Main activity on the phone app (filename: /mobile/src/main/java/. . ./ MyActivityPhone.java)

```java
package com.wiley.wrox.chapter7.wearabledatafromscratch;

import […]

public class MyActivityPhone extends Activity {

    private GoogleApiClient mGoogleApiClient;
    private int mColorCount = 0;
    private BroadcastReceiver mResultReceiver;
    @Override
    protected void onCreate(Bundle savedInstanceState) {
        super.onCreate(savedInstanceState);
        setContentView(R.layout.activity_my_phone);

        mGoogleApiClient = new GoogleApiClient.Builder(this)
                .addConnectionCallbacks(new GoogleApiClient.ConnectionCallbacks() {
                    @Override
                    public void onConnected(Bundle connectionHint) {
                        Log.v("wrox-mobile", "Connection established");
                    }
                    @Override
                    public void onConnectionSuspended(int cause) {
                        Log.v("wrox-mobile", "Connection suspended");
                    }
                })
                .addOnConnectionFailedListener(new
GoogleApiClient.OnConnectionFailedListener() {
                    @Override
                    public void onConnectionFailed(ConnectionResult result) {
                        Log.v("wrox-mobile", "Connection failed");
                    }
                })
                .addApi(Wearable.API)
                .build();
        mGoogleApiClient.connect();

        mResultReceiver = createBroadcastReceiver();
        LocalBroadcastManager.getInstance(this).registerReceiver(
                mResultReceiver,
                new IntentFilter("phone.localIntent"));

    }

    […]
```

```
    public void syncDataItem(View view) {
        if(mGoogleApiClient==null)
            return;

        int r = (int) (255 * Math.random());
        int g = (int) (255 * Math.random());
        int b = (int) (255 * Math.random());

        final PutDataMapRequest putRequest =
PutDataMapRequest.create("/PHONE2WEAR");
        final DataMap map = putRequest.getDataMap();
        map.putInt("color", Color.rgb(r,g,b));
        map.putString("colorChanges", "Amount of changes: " + mColorCount++);
        Wearable.DataApi.putDataItem(mGoogleApiClient,
putRequest.asPutDataRequest());

        Log.v("wrox-mobile", "Handheld sent new random color to watch");
        Log.v("wrox-mobile", "color:" + r + ", " + g + ", " + b);
        Log.v("wrox-mobile", "iteration:" + mColorCount);
    }

    private void updateTextField(String text) {
        Log.v("wrox-mobile", "Arrived text:" + text);
        ((TextView)findViewById(R.id.reply_text)).setText(text);
    }

    @Override
    protected void onDestroy() {
        if (mResultReceiver != null) {
            LocalBroadcastManager.getInstance(this)
                .unregisterReceiver(mResultReceiver);
        }
        super.onDestroy();
    }

    private BroadcastReceiver createBroadcastReceiver() {
        return new BroadcastReceiver() {
            @Override
            public void onReceive(Context context, Intent intent) {
                updateTextField(intent.getStringExtra("result"));
            }
        };
    }

}
```

The Phone's AndroidManifest.xml

Listing 7-10 shows the manifest file for the phone. I've highlighted the service declaration. Together with the metadata tag declaring the use of the Google Play services API, these are the two changes needed for the service to boot when the app launches and for the combo to use the Google API to talk to the other device.

LISTING 7-10: Full manifest file (filename: `/mobile/src/main/AndroidManifest.xml`)

```xml
<?xml version="1.0" encoding="utf-8"?>
<manifest xmlns:android="http://schemas.android.com/apk/res/android"
    package="com.wiley.wrox.chapter7.wearabledatafromscratch" >

    <application
        android:allowBackup="true"
        android:icon="@drawable/wrox_logo_big"
        android:label="@string/app_name"
        android:theme="@style/AppTheme" >
        <activity
            android:name=".MyActivityPhone"
            android:label="@string/app_name" >
            <intent-filter>
                <action android:name="android.intent.action.MAIN" />

                <category android:name="android.intent.category.LAUNCHER" />
            </intent-filter>
        </activity>

        <service android:name=".DataLayerListenerServicePhone" >
            <intent-filter>
                <action android:name=
                    "com.google.android.gms.wearable.BIND_LISTENER" />
            </intent-filter>
        </service>

        <meta-data android:name="com.google.android.gms.version"
            android:value="@integer/google_play_services_version" />

    </application>
</manifest>
```

The Phone's DataLayerListenerService

`DataLayerListenerService` is launched on the phone after the app launches. When the phone registers an event of any of the shared data objects changing, the listener is triggered. In this case it filters by WEAR2PHONE. This object, as defined in MyActivityWear.java (check the source code later in the chapter), carries two float numbers—the x-coordinate and the y-coordinate of the last time the screen was touched.

In Listing 7-11 you can see the listener service in the phone that will be waiting for the wearable device to make changes on the shared data object.

LISTING 7-11: Listener on the phone (filename: `/mobile/src/main/java/.../DataLayerListenerServicePhone.java`)

```java
public class DataLayerListenerServicePhone extends WearableListenerService {

    @Override
```

```java
public void onDataChanged(DataEventBuffer dataEvents) {
    super.onDataChanged(dataEvents);

    Log.v("wrox-mobile", "Data arrived");

    final List<DataEvent> events = FreezableUtils.freezeIterable(dataEvents);
    for(DataEvent event : events) {
        final Uri uri = event.getDataItem().getUri();
        final String path = uri!=null ? uri.getPath() : null;
        if("/WEAR2PHONE".equals(path)) {
            final DataMap map = DataMapItem
                .fromDataItem(event.getDataItem()).getDataMap();
            // read your values from map:
            float X = map.getFloat("touchX");
            float Y = map.getFloat("touchY");
            String reply = "Touched X=" + X + ", Y=" + Y;
            Log.v("wrox-mobile", reply);
            Intent localIntent = new Intent("phone.localIntent");
            localIntent.putExtra("result", reply);
            LocalBroadcastManager.getInstance(this)
                .sendBroadcast(localIntent);
        }
    }
}
```

> **NOTE** *You don't need a Wear device to test these apps. As you will see later in this chapter, I used the emulator for the watch. To simulate touches on the screen, simply use the mouse pointer and click over the interface.*

MyActivityWear.java

The activity on the watch is very similar to the one on the phone. Just take a look at Listing 7-12, a snippet of the main class running on the phone. You will see that it is more or less the same application as on the phone, with these differences:

➤ In this case the data is sent as WEAR2PHONE.

➤ The property we are changing in this case is the background color—a combo of the setActivityBackgroundColor() and setBackgroundColor() methods.

➤ touchListener is implemented within the method dedicated to the layout. Because the listener is responsible for detecting touches and sending them, all the needed code is added there, inline.

LISTING 7-12: Main activity class on the wearable (filename: /wear/src/main/
java/. . .MainActivityWear.java)

```java
package com.wiley.wrox.chapter7.wearabledatafromscratch;

import […]

public class MyActivityWear extends Activity {

    private GoogleApiClient mGoogleApiClient;
    private TextView mTextView;
    private int mColor;
    private BroadcastReceiver mResultReceiver;

    @Override
    protected void onCreate(Bundle savedInstanceState) {
        super.onCreate(savedInstanceState);
        setContentView(R.layout.activity_my_wear);

        mGoogleApiClient = new GoogleApiClient.Builder(this)
                .addConnectionCallbacks(new GoogleApiClient
                        .ConnectionCallbacks() {
                    @Override
                    public void onConnected(Bundle connectionHint) {
                        Log.v("wrox-wear", "Connection established");
                    }
                    @Override
                    public void onConnectionSuspended(int cause) {
                        Log.v("wrox-wear", "Connection suspended");
                    }
                })
                .addOnConnectionFailedListener(new GoogleApiClient
                        .OnConnectionFailedListener() {
                    @Override
                    public void onConnectionFailed(ConnectionResult result) {
                        Log.v("wrox-wear", "Connection failed");
                    }
                })
                .addApi(Wearable.API)
                .build();
        mGoogleApiClient.connect();

        final WatchViewStub stub = (WatchViewStub)
            findViewById(R.id.watch_view_stub);
        stub.setOnLayoutInflatedListener(new
            WatchViewStub.OnLayoutInflatedListener() {
            @Override
            public void onLayoutInflated(WatchViewStub stub) {
                mTextView = (TextView) stub.findViewById(R.id.text);

                stub.setOnTouchListener(new View.OnTouchListener() {
                    @Override
                    public boolean onTouch(View view, MotionEvent event) {
```

```java
                    String s = "X=" + event.getX();
                    s += ", Y=" + event.getY();
                    Log.v("wrox-wear", s);

                    if(mGoogleApiClient==null)
                        return false;

                    final PutDataMapRequest putRequest =
                        PutDataMapRequest.create("/WEAR2PHONE");
                    final DataMap map = putRequest.getDataMap();
                    map.putFloat("touchX", event.getX());
                    map.putFloat("touchY", event.getY());
                    Wearable.DataApi.putDataItem(mGoogleApiClient,
                        putRequest.asPutDataRequest());

                    return false;
                }
            });
        }
    });

    mResultReceiver = createBroadcastReceiver();
    LocalBroadcastManager.getInstance(this).registerReceiver(
            mResultReceiver,
            new IntentFilter("wearable.localIntent"));
}

private void setBackgroundColor(int color) {
    Log.v("wrox-wear", "Arrived color:" + color);
    final WatchViewStub stub = (WatchViewStub)
        findViewById(R.id.watch_view_stub);
    stub.setBackgroundColor(color);
}

@Override
protected void onDestroy() {
    if (mResultReceiver != null) {
        LocalBroadcastManager.getInstance(this)
            .unregisterReceiver(mResultReceiver);
    }
    super.onDestroy();
}

private BroadcastReceiver createBroadcastReceiver() {
    return new BroadcastReceiver() {
        @Override
        public void onReceive(Context context, Intent intent) {
            setBackgroundColor(
intent.getIntExtra("result"));
        }
    };
}
}
```

Wear's Android Manifest File

Listing 7-13 shows that there is almost no difference between the manifest file for the wearable and the one for the handheld.

LISTING 7-13: Main activity class on the wearable (filename: /wear/src/main/ AndroidManifest.xml)

```xml
<?xml version="1.0" encoding="utf-8"?>
<manifest xmlns:android="http://schemas.android.com/apk/res/android"
    package="com.wiley.wrox.chapter7.wearabledatafromscratch" >

    <uses-feature android:name="android.hardware.type.watch" />

    <application
        android:allowBackup="true"
        android:icon="@drawable/ic_launcher"
        android:label="@string/app_name"
        android:theme="@android:style/Theme.DeviceDefault" >
        <activity
            android:name=".MyActivityWear"
            android:label="@string/app_name" >
            <intent-filter>
                <action android:name="android.intent.action.MAIN" />

                <category android:name="android.intent.category.LAUNCHER" />
            </intent-filter>
        </activity>

        <service android:name=".DataLayerListenerServiceWear" >
            <intent-filter>
                <action android:name=
                    "com.google.android.gms.wearable.BIND_LISTENER" />
            </intent-filter>
        </service>

        <meta-data android:name="com.google.android.gms.version"
            android:value="@integer/google_play_services_version" />
    </application>

</manifest>
```

The Listener on the Wearable's Side

Listing 7-14 shows the last piece of the puzzle.

LISTING 7-14: Wearable's listener (filename: /wear/src/main/java/.../ DataLayerListenerServiceWear.java)

```java
public class DataLayerListenerServiceWear extends WearableListenerService {

    @Override
```

```java
public void onDataChanged(DataEventBuffer dataEvents) {
    super.onDataChanged(dataEvents);

    Log.v("wrox-wear", "Data arrived");

    final List<DataEvent> events = FreezableUtils
        .freezeIterable(dataEvents);
    for(DataEvent event : events) {
        final Uri uri = event.getDataItem().getUri();
        final String path = uri!=null ? uri.getPath() : null;
        if("/PHONE2WEAR".equals(path)) {
            final DataMap map = DataMapItem
                .fromDataItem(event.getDataItem()).getDataMap();
            // read your values from map:
            int color = map.getInt("color");
            Log.v("wrox-wear", "Color received: " + color);

            Intent localIntent = new Intent("wearable.localIntent");
            localIntent.putExtra("result", color);
            LocalBroadcastManager.getInstance(this)
                .sendBroadcast(localIntent);

            String colorChanges = map.getString("colorChanges");
            Log.v("wrox-wear", colorChanges);
        }
    }
}
```

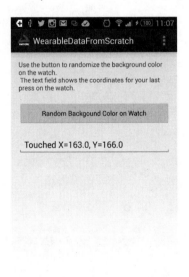

FIGURE 7-4: The Data transmission
app on a phone

The Final Result

I haven't focused on showing the layout for either of the
applications. I recommend you check the full example on the
book's downloads under chapter7_WearableDataFromScratch
.zip. There you will find all the code used here, ready for you to
copy and start experimenting with in your own applications.

The expected result on your side should be something like what
is shown in the next two figures. Figure 7-4 is a screenshot of
the activity on my phone. Figure 7-5 is a screenshot of the watch
after the button on the phone's UI is pressed and the watch's
screen is touched.

FIGURE 7-5: The watch after
the screen changes color

SUMMARY

This chapter has shown you how to run the basic Wearable API communication example provided by Google in the Android Wear SDK. You have learned how to make your own simple, bidirectional app ecosystem so that you can share data records between apps on different devices.

Remember that the way to communicate between your handheld and your watch is Google Play services.

In the next chapter you'll explore how to stream audio over Bluetooth.

RECOMMENDED READING

Visit the following documentation sites from the Android Wear project for further reference:
- `https://developer.android.com/training/wearables/data-layer/accessing.html`
- `https://developer.android.com/training/wearables/data-layer/data-items.html`

Location-Based Services on Android Wear

WROX.COM CODE DOWNLOADS FOR THIS CHAPTER

The wrox.com code downloads for this chapter are found at www.wrox.com/go/androidwearables on the Download Code tab. The code is in the Chapter 8 download, and the files are named according to the listing numbers noted throughout the chapter.

CHANGING HOW LOCATION WORKS

With the release of the updated Android Wear system in late October 2014, using a global positioning system (GPS) in your Wear apps became technically possible. The Sony SmartWatch 3, the first device that sported the required hardware, was released in late November.

Because the Wear devices are often connected to a master device, the phone, there is always the possibility of accessing the phone's sensor data. This possibility has forced Google to review how the GPS libraries work on Wear. Previously you would ask the Android system (android.location) for the most suitable location provider according to your specific requirements. In Wear you instead use the newer Google Services location API (gms.location) to access the location services.

Apart from handling location updates in Android Wear, the Google Play location API gives you a handful of other interesting features, including detecting your user's physical activity, such as walking or running. It also has helper classes for interacting with geographic areas (geofences).

Accessing the Current Location

To access anything location-based in Android Wear, you need to use the `FusedLocationProvider` class, which selects the most appropriate GPS provider on your device(s). This new API is much simpler in terms of readable code. It's also more power-efficient, because it considers other apps' location update requests.

Another feature of `FusedLocationProvider` is the combination of multiple GPS sensors. Because your Wear device may or may not have a GPS sensor built in, the system needs a way to figure out which sensor is the best option for your needs. In most cases when the Wear device is connected to your phone, it chooses to read updates directly from the phone instead, thereby saving battery on the Wear device. If the phone and Wear device are not connected, the system requests updates directly from the built-in GPS sensor.

Enabling GPS support

Start by requesting permission to use the location services. There are two levels available: `ACCESS_FINE_LOCATION` and `ACCESS_COARSE_LOCATION`. If you want to use the GPS radio you'll need to add the `ACCESS_FINE_LOCATION` location. Open the manifest and add the lines shown in Listing 8-1.

LISTING 8-1: Requesting GPS permission

```xml
<?xml version="1.0" encoding="utf-8"?>
<manifest xmlns:android="http://schemas.android.com/apk/res/android"
    package="com.wiley.wrox.myapplication" >

    <uses-feature android:name="android.hardware.type.watch" />

    <uses-permission android:name="android.permission.ACCESS_FINE_LOCATION" />
    ...

</manifest>
```

Using the New APIs

Before you can access `FusedLocationProvider`, you need to establish a connection using `GoogleApiClient`. Connect to the Wear activity in your `onCreate` method using the code shown in Listing 8-2.

When you're working with location through Google Services, the same rules apply as with any other API. Use `ConnectionCallbacks` to get information about your connection attempt status, and handle failed connection attempts in `OnConnectionFailedListener`.

LISTING 8-2: Creating GoogleApiClient

```java
package com.wiley.wrox.gpsproject;

import android.app.Activity;
import android.os.Bundle;
import android.support.wearable.view.WatchViewStub;
import android.widget.TextView;

import com.google.android.gms.common.api.GoogleApiClient;
import com.google.android.gms.location.LocationServices;

public class WearActivity extends Activity {

  private TextView mTextView;

  private GoogleApiClient mApiClient;

  @Override
  protected void onCreate(Bundle savedInstanceState) {
    super.onCreate(savedInstanceState);
    setContentView(R.layout.activity_wear);
    final WatchViewStub stub = (WatchViewStub) findViewById(R.id.watch_view_stub);
    stub.setOnLayoutInflatedListener(new WatchViewStub.OnLayoutInflatedListener() {
      @Override
      public void onLayoutInflated(WatchViewStub stub) {
        mTextView = (TextView) stub.findViewById(R.id.text);
      }
    });

    mApiClient = new GoogleApiClient.Builder(this)
        .addApi(LocationServices.API)
        .addConnectionCallbacks(mConnectionListener)
        .addOnConnectionFailedListener(mConnectionFailedListener)
        .build();
  }

  @Override
  protected void onResume() {
    super.onResume();
  }

  @Override
  protected void onPause() {
    super.onPause();
  }

}
```

Add the connection callbacks, and then request a connection to Google Services from within the onResume life-cycle method, as shown in Listing 8-3. Don't forget to also add the disconnect call in onPause.

LISTING 8-3: Adding the callbacks and connecting

```java
package com.wiley.wrox.gpsproject;

import android.app.Activity;
import android.location.Location;
import android.os.Bundle;
import android.support.wearable.view.WatchViewStub;
import android.widget.TextView;

import com.google.android.gms.common.ConnectionResult;
import com.google.android.gms.common.api.GoogleApiClient;
import com.google.android.gms.location.LocationServices;

public class WearActivity extends Activity {

  private TextView mTextView;

  private GoogleApiClient mApiClient;

  @Override
  protected void onCreate(Bundle savedInstanceState) {
    super.onCreate(savedInstanceState);
    setContentView(R.layout.activity_wear);
    final WatchViewStub stub = (WatchViewStub) findViewById(R.id.watch_view_stub);
    stub.setOnLayoutInflatedListener(new WatchViewStub.OnLayoutInflatedListener() {
      @Override
      public void onLayoutInflated(WatchViewStub stub) {
        mTextView = (TextView) stub.findViewById(R.id.text);
      }
    });

    mApiClient = new GoogleApiClient.Builder(this)
        .addApi(LocationServices.API)
        .addApi(Wearable.API)
        .addConnectionCallbacks(mConnectionListener)
        .addOnConnectionFailedListener(mConnectionFailedListener)
        .build();
  }

  @Override
  protected void onResume() {
    super.onResume();
    mApiClient.connect();
  }

  @Override
  protected void onPause() {
    super.onPause();
    mApiClient.disconnect();
  }

  private GoogleApiClient.ConnectionCallbacks mConnectionListener = new
      GoogleApiClient.ConnectionCallbacks() {
```

```
        @Override
        public void onConnected(Bundle bundle) {
        }

        @Override
        public void onConnectionSuspended(int i) {
        }
    };

    private GoogleApiClient.OnConnectionFailedListener mConnectionFailedListener =
        new GoogleApiClient.OnConnectionFailedListener() {
        @Override
        public void onConnectionFailed(ConnectionResult connectionResult) {
        }
    };
}
```

Determining GPS Availability

Although connecting to the Google Services Client is no problem, suppose the Wear device has no built-in GPS. Listing 8-4 shows how to check for support for GPS.

LISTING 8-4: Detecting if a device has a GPS sensor

```
private boolean hasGpsSupport(){
  return getPackageManager().hasSystemFeature(PackageManager
    .FEATURE_LOCATION_GPS);
}
```

This is, of course, also possible by using the uses-feature element in your application manifest, effectively limiting what devices can install your application.

Requesting the Last Known Location

To request the last known location, you use the FusedLocationApi class. You can find it within LocationServices, as shown in Listing 8-5. Make sure to call this only when the device has connected to Google Services.

LISTING 8-5: Getting the last known location

```
private GoogleApiClient.ConnectionCallbacks mConnectionListener = new
  GoogleApiClient.ConnectionCallbacks() {
    @Override
    public void onConnected(Bundle bundle) {
      Location loc = LocationServices.FusedLocationApi.getLastLocation
        (mApiClient);
      if (loc != null) {
        mTextView.setText(loc.getLatitude() + ", " + loc.getLongitude());
```

continues

LISTING 8-5: *(continued)*

```
        }
    }

    @Override
    public void onConnectionSuspended(int i) {
    }
};
```

This particular call may throw a `NullPointerException` and cause the app to crash sometimes. It all depends on the current state of the GPS. This is because `LocationService` still has not received an updated location. There are two ways to deal with this problem. Either you wait with the request for the latest update, or you register a `LocationListener` for a single location update. The second option may be a bit more secure, because it never delivers a null value. However, it also may never deliver a value at all. In that case you should set an expiration for your request (as described in Table 8-1).

TABLE 8-1: Location Request Options

OPTION	DESCRIPTION
Priority	Describes the general urgency of your location updates. You can choose from `PRIORITY_HIGH_ACCURACY`, `PRIORITY_BALANCED_POWER_ACCURACY`, `PRIORITY_LOW_POWER`, and `PRIORITY_NO_POWER`. `HIGH` is the most accurate, `BALANCED` is "block"-level accuracy, `LOW POWER` is "city"-level accuracy, and `NO POWER` is as good as possible without consuming any power.
Expiration	Sets the expiration of the location. There are two methods for setting the expiration. `setExpirationDuration(long)` sets the amount of time the request lives, and `setExpirationTime(long)` sets the exact expiration time since the device booted.
Interval	Sets the desired rate (in milliseconds) for location updates. You should consider this a wish, not a promise. Sometimes you may not receive any updates.
Fastest interval	Sets the limit of how fast your app receives location updates. Unlike the normal interval, this value is exact, meaning your app can receive updates faster than the GPS provides them. This can be handy when you want to receive many updates while still conserving power.
Number of updates	Defines the number of location updates you want your app to receive. When using this setting, you should also be sure to set the expiration time of your request. If you don't, your request might live forever, consuming valuable battery power.
Smallest displacement	Sets the minimum distance between location updates in meters. The default value is 0.

Requesting Location Updates

Sometimes it's not enough to have just one location update. You may need more frequent updates on the location. In those cases you use `LocationListener`. Listing 8-6 shows how to attach a listener and request periodic updates.

LISTING 8-6: Requesting periodic location updates

```java
package com.wiley.wrox.gpsproject;

import android.app.Activity;
import android.content.pm.PackageManager;
import android.location.Location;
import android.os.Bundle;
import android.support.wearable.view.WatchViewStub;
import android.widget.TextView;

import com.google.android.gms.common.ConnectionResult;
import com.google.android.gms.common.api.GoogleApiClient;
import com.google.android.gms.location.LocationListener;
import com.google.android.gms.location.LocationRequest;
import com.google.android.gms.location.LocationServices;

public class WearActivity extends Activity {

  private TextView mTextView;

  private GoogleApiClient mApiClient;

  @Override
  protected void onCreate(Bundle savedInstanceState) {
    super.onCreate(savedInstanceState);
    setContentView(R.layout.activity_wear);
    final WatchViewStub stub = (WatchViewStub) findViewById(R.id.watch_view_stub);
    stub.setOnLayoutInflatedListener(new WatchViewStub.OnLayoutInflatedListener() {
      @Override
      public void onLayoutInflated(WatchViewStub stub) {
        mTextView = (TextView) stub.findViewById(R.id.text);
      }
    });

    mApiClient = new GoogleApiClient.Builder(this)
        .addApi(LocationServices.API)
        .addConnectionCallbacks(mConnectionListener)
        .addOnConnectionFailedListener(mConnectionFailedListener)
        .build();
  }

  @Override
  protected void onResume() {
    super.onResume();
    mApiClient.connect();
  }

  @Override
  protected void onPause() {
    super.onPause();
    LocationServices.FusedLocationApi.removeLocationUpdates(mApiClient,
        mLocationListener);
    mApiClient.disconnect();
```

```
        }

        private GoogleApiClient.ConnectionCallbacks mConnectionListener = new
            GoogleApiClient.ConnectionCallbacks() {
                @Override
                public void onConnected(Bundle bundle) {
                    LocationRequest request = LocationRequest.create();
                    LocationServices.FusedLocationApi.requestLocationUpdates(mApiClient, request,
                        mLocationListener);
                }

                @Override
                public void onConnectionSuspended(int i) {
                }
            };

        private GoogleApiClient.OnConnectionFailedListener mConnectionFailedListener =
            new GoogleApiClient.OnConnectionFailedListener() {
                @Override
                public void onConnectionFailed(ConnectionResult connectionResult) {
                }
            };

        private LocationListener mLocationListener = new LocationListener() {
          @Override
          public void onLocationChanged(Location location) {
            mTextView.setText(location.getLatitude() + ", " + location.getLongitude());
          }
        };
    }
```

When either the request for the latest location or the request for periodic location updates returns a location, your app should look something like Figure 8-1.

Being Picky About Location Updates

Requesting a default location update works just fine, but in most cases you may want to be pickier about how you request your updates. If you request updates too seldom, your app may not be as functional as you want. If you request too often, the battery life may be significantly reduced. Neither option is good.

FIGURE 8-1: Displaying GPS coordinates on the device

To make more sense of your location updates, you can set multiple options, as shown in Table 8-1.

These options are set through an equal number of setter methods. Each setter returns a new LocationRequest object, meaning you can chain these values as shown in Listing 8-7.

LISTING 8-7: Setting location request options

```
    private GoogleApiClient.ConnectionCallbacks mConnectionListener = new
        GoogleApiClient.ConnectionCallbacks() {
```

```
    @Override
    public void onConnected(Bundle bundle) {
        LocationRequest request = LocationRequest.create()
            .setPriority(LocationRequest.PRIORITY_BALANCED_POWER_ACCURACY)
            .setExpirationDuration(2000)
            .setFastestInterval(500)
            .setInterval(2000)
            .setNumUpdates(2)
            .setSmallestDisplacement(0.5f);

        LocationServices.FusedLocationApi.requestLocationUpdates(mApiClient,
            request, mLocationListener);
    }

    @Override
    public void onConnectionSuspended(int i) {
    }
};
```

This request has balanced ("block"-level) accuracy and power consumption. It expires after 2 seconds and delivers location updates twice per second. It delivers a maximum of two location updates, and the user must move at least half a meter before a new location update is delivered.

Showing Your Street Address

While latitude and longitude (and any other values the location may give you) are very handy, in some cases they're just not good enough. Sometimes you want your locations to be in a human-readable format. That's when you need to apply reverse geocoding to your location.

Luckily a service called Geocoder exists for this exact purpose. However, it's not available on all devices, so you must be sure to check if this service is available before you attempt to use it.

Testing Geocoder Availability

Use the helper method isPresent() as shown in Listing 8-8 to test if Geocoder is present.

LISTING 8-8: Testing if Geocoder is present

```
private LocationListener mLocationListener = new LocationListener() {
    @Override
    public void onLocationChanged(Location location) {
        if(Geocoder.isPresent()){
        }
    }
};
```

Getting the Current Address for a Location

Before you can translate the location to an address, you need to create the Geocoder instance. However, because the Geocoder service is running synchronously, you should wrap this in a thread. Listing 8-9 shows you how.

LISTING 8-9: Creating a Geocoder instance

```java
private LocationListener mLocationListener = new LocationListener() {
  @Override
  public void onLocationChanged(Location location) {
    if (Geocoder.isPresent()) {
      new AsyncTask<Double, Void, Address>() {
        @Override
        protected Address doInBackground(Double...doubles) {
          Geocoder coder = new Geocoder(WearActivity.this, Locale.getDefault());
          return null;
        }
      }.execute(location.getLatitude(), location.getLongitude());
    }
  }
};
```

The `Geocoder` object returns a list of possible addresses for the location you look up. Create a list of `Address` objects, and call the method `getFromLocation(double, double, int)`, passing the latitude and longitude and the number of results you're interested in. We'll accept only a single result this time, so pass a 1 (see Listing 8-10).

LISTING 8-10: Getting the most accurate address

```java
private LocationListener mLocationListener = new LocationListener() {
  @Override
  public void onLocationChanged(Location location) {
    if (Geocoder.isPresent()) {
      new AsyncTask<Double, Void, Address>() {
        @Override
        protected Address doInBackground(Double...doubles) {
          Geocoder coder = new Geocoder(WearActivity.this, Locale.getDefault());
          List<Address> addressList = null;
          try {
            addressList = coder.getFromLocation(doubles[0], doubles[1], 1);
            if (addressList != null && addressList.size() > 0) {
              return addressList.get(0);
            }
          } catch (IOException e) {
            e.printStackTrace();
          }
          return null;
        }
      }.execute(location.getLatitude(), location.getLongitude());
    }
  }
};
```

Since we're doing the reverse geocoding outside of the UI thread, we need to be sure to post the address when we're back on the UI thread. Luckily `AsyncTask` has a method just for this called `onPostExecute()`.

If `Geocoder` is not available on your Wear device, you should use the data APIs to have the phone look up the address.

SUMMARY

In this chapter you explored the "new" Google location services. In particular, you tested them on the new Android Wear platform.

You read the last known location and started reading recurring location updates with `LocationListener`. You finished the chapter by looking at reverse geocoding and activity recognition. All in all, you covered most of the location services available in Android.

This is the final chapter in Part II of the book. Part III contains a few interesting projects that dive a bit deeper into real-life contexts for wearable apps.

RECOMMENDED READING

More in-depth information about how the GPS works, `http://en.wikipedia.org/wiki/Global_Positioning_System`

Android Location APIs can be found at `https://developer.android.com/google/play-services/location.html`

PART III
Projects

Android Wear as Activity Tracker

WHAT'S IN THIS CHAPTER?

➤ Introduction to activity trackers

➤ Working with sensors on Wear

➤ Displaying data on small screens

WROX.COM CODE DOWNLOADS FOR THIS CHAPTER

The code downloads for this chapter are found at www.wrox.com/go/androidwearables on the Download Code tab. The code is in the Chapter 9 download and the files are individually named according to the listing numbers noted throughout the chapter.

WHAT ARE ACTIVITY TRACKERS?

Activity Trackers, as their name implies, are sensors that we wear on our bodies or in our hands to store data about our physical activities so that we can later review the statistics. A 2009 article published in the Harvard Health Letter stated that pedometers increase our physical activity by motivating us to achieve simple goals such as taking 10,000 steps every day.

There are several different kinds of Activity Trackers. Some have simple functionality, and others have more-complex combinations of sensors. Special apps for your smartphone can do the same things as a dedicated Activity Tracker. The past few years these devices and apps have risen steadily in popularity among regular people. Professional athletes have used them for quite some time. For example, an Activity Tracker can be used to collect a football player's statistics during games with the goal of maximizing his output on the field.

A number of devices are available for people who enjoy sports as a hobby, not a profession. These include the Nike+ FuelBand, the Sony SmartBand, and the Gear Fit from Samsung. Another popular brand is Fitbit, which has, to this author's knowledge, three different devices aimed at different types of practitioners. Of course, these are just a few of the available ones. Describing all their differences is beyond the scope of this chapter. We'll explore how to create your own basic Activity Tracker application for Android Wear.

WEAR AS AN ACTIVITY TRACKER

The typical Android Wear device is basically the same as an Activity Tracker, only packaged in a slightly different way. Android Wear devices already have the core sensors required to measure activity. And because the device usually is connected to your phone, it can access all the phone's resources and sensors as well, making it a powerful—although bloated—competitor to the dedicated devices.

FIGURE 9-1: The Fit app

In fact, Android Wear devices come packaged with a simple Activity Tracker app called Fit, as shown in Figure 9-1. It doesn't offer anything near the complexity of a real Activity Tracker device, but it's a decent starting point if you want to become more physically active without having to sign up for a gym membership.

The Fit app uses the new sensors introduced with Android Kit Kat (API 19) called Step Detector and Step Counter. They're a new breed of power-efficient composite sensors that use a special hardware sensor based on an accelerometer to detect when the user has taken a step.

The new sensor is good at determining when a step has been taken. It works for walking, running, and climbing stairs. It also attempts to ignore when you're driving or when you're riding a bike or train.

Step Detector

The Step Detector, as its name implies, triggers when the person wearing the smartwatch takes a step. This sensor can deliver results to the user fairly quickly. On the other hand, it has a rather high rate of false positives, meaning it can trigger a step detection even when the user hasn't taken a step.

This rate of false positives can be minimized by applying another new feature of Kit Kat—batching sensor values. Batching does not remove any sensor readings, but it delivers them with some delay. Doing so conserves power and may improve readings.

The Step Detector sensor doesn't require any special permissions, but because it's a sensor that requires special hardware, it's highly recommended that you include a uses-feature in your manifest if you plan on working with it. See Listing 9-1.

LISTING 9-1: Adding the uses-feature element for the Step Detector

```
<uses-feature android:name="android.hardware.sensor.stepdetector" />
```

Step Counter

Much like the Step Detector, the Step Counter uses the new hardware sensor introduced in Kit Kat. The big difference between the counter and the detector is how they work. The Step Detector delivers uncertain values at a high pace, and the Step Counter delivers more certain values at a low pace.

The value Step Counter delivers is the accumulated number of steps taken since the device booted up. So if your device has been "alive" for a long time without rebooting, this value may be very high.

Just like the Step Detector, this sensor requires special hardware. Therefore, you should add the `uses-feature` shown in Listing 9-2.

LISTING 9-2: The uses-feature element for Step Counter

```
<uses-feature android:name="android.hardware.sensor.stepcounter" />
```

These new sensors were introduced in Kit Kat (API 19), but because you're using them on a Wear device (API 20, or 4.4W), you don't need to change the minimum required SDK.

You're now ready to begin building your own Activity Tracker using Android Wear. You'll make a simple app called WalkKeeper for people who enjoy walking for exercise.

> **NOTE** *Technically, the hardware required for the steps sensors aren't new per se. It's an extra, very power-efficient processor dedicated to reading and interpreting the data coming in from the activity sensors, such as the accelerometer. It's very similar to the Apple co-processors (M7) motion processor which was introduced with iPhone 5S.*

BUILDING THE WALKKEEPER APP

The WalkKeeper app, while active, tracks how many calories are burned by walking, and it does so live. First you must establish a basic algorithm for calculating how many calories are burned when walking. This can easily become a fairly complex equation, but we'll keep it simple in this example and let you think about developing something more complex on your own.

Calculating Calories

You should consider several variables when calculating calories consumed by physical activities. Height, weight, gender, and number of steps taken are all integral parts of the equation, as shown in Table 9-1.

TABLE 9-1: Variables for Calculating Calories

VARIABLE	LETTER(S)	DESCRIPTION
Stride Factor	SF	This is important because you'll work a lot with averages in your app to simplify the interface. Assume that the average woman has an average walking stride of 0.413 times her height and that the average male has an average stride of 0.415 times his height.
Height	H	This value, in centimeters, is needed to calculate the average stride length.
Steps	S	This is the core of the app. The number of steps is needed to calculate how far the user has traveled.
Weight	W	This value, in kilograms, is needed to calculate how many calories are burned with each mile the user walks.

Given these variables, the equations for calculating the Stride Length (SL), in centimeters, look like this:

$$SL = H \times SF \text{ (cm)}$$

To get the total distance (D) travelled you use the stride length (SL) and the number of steps (S) taken by the user. Because the stride length is in centimeters you should also convert it to kilometers:

$$D = SL \times S \times 0.00001 \text{ (km)}$$

Here's the equation for calculating the calories burned per distance (CBD) in kilometers:

$$CBD = W \times 2.02 \text{ (Cal/km)}$$

> **NOTE** *I use a factor of 2.02 because many health websites use this value to calculate calories burned when someone walks at an average speed. This is, of course, a very simplistic formula, which in reality consists of many more variables such as how fast you're walking, how steep the path is, wind direction and strength, and more.*

Here's the equation for calculating the total number of calories burned (TCB) based on the number of steps the user takes:

$$TCB = CBD \times D \text{ (Cal)}$$

If you apply the equations for calories burned per distance (CBD) and distance (D) you'll get the following equation:

$$TCB = (W \times 2.02) \times (SL \times S \times 0.00001) \text{ (Cal)}$$

Finally, apply the equation for calculation of stride length (SL) and you'll end up with a simplified equation for calculating the calories burned based on your weight, height, and the number of steps you've taken:

$$TCB = (W \times 2.02) \times (H \times SF \times S \times 0.00001) \text{ (Cal)}$$

Creating the Project

Begin by creating a new project:

1. Call it **WalkKeeper** and enter the company domain, wrox.wiley.com.

2. Check both the Wear and the Phone and Tablet check boxes.

3. Choose Blank Activity to create a blank activity for mobile, and call it **WalkKeeperActivity**. We won't actually use this activity in the example, but it's good to have it for future developments.

4. Choose Blank Activity to create a blank activity for Wear, and call it **SelectGenderActivity**. This will be the starting activity on the Wear device.

5. Click Finish, and open your newly created `SelectGenderActivity` class.

Selecting Gender

The first activity we require in this application is a way to select a gender. We'll use `WearableListView` for this purpose. Open the two layouts for your `SelectGenderActivity` activity—`rect_activity_select_gender.xml` and `round_activity_select_gender.xml`—and add the `WearableListView` element. Listing 9-3 shows the layout for the rectangular device. The round layout is pretty much identical; we're not showing it here.

LISTING 9-3: Building the user interface for selecting a gender

```xml
<?xml version="1.0" encoding="utf-8"?>
<LinearLayout
    xmlns:android="http://schemas.android.com/apk/res/android"
    xmlns:tools="http://schemas.android.com/tools"
    android:layout_width="match_parent"
    android:layout_height="match_parent"
    android:orientation="vertical"
    tools:context=".SelectGenderActivity"
    tools:deviceIds="wear_square">

  <android.support.wearable.view.WearableListView
    android:id="@+id/list"
    android:layout_width="match_parent"
    android:layout_height="match_parent"/>
</LinearLayout>
```

Switch to `SelectGenderActivity` and load `WearableListView` from the layout. We're using the standard `Activity` class, so remember to use `WatchViewStub.OnLayoutInflatedListener` to attach the correct UI widgets. Listing 9-4 shows you how.

LISTING 9-4: Beginning SelectGenderActivity

```
package com.wiley.wrox.walkkeeper;

import android.app.Activity;
import android.os.Bundle;
import android.support.wearable.view.WatchViewStub;
import android.support.wearable.view.WearableListView;

public class SelectGenderActivity extends Activity {

  private WearableListView mListView;

  @Override
  protected void onCreate(Bundle savedInstanceState) {
    super.onCreate(savedInstanceState);
    setContentView(R.layout.activity_select_gender);
    final WatchViewStub stub = (WatchViewStub) findViewById(R.id.watch_view_stub);
    stub.setOnLayoutInflatedListener(new WatchViewStub.OnLayoutInflatedListener() {
      @Override
      public void onLayoutInflated(WatchViewStub stub) {
        mListView = (WearableListView) stub.findViewById(R.id.list);
      }
    });
  }
}
```

Next we create the adapter class. In Wear, adapters are simple. Everything is included, including the view holder pattern. So we just need to fill the adapter with the data, which is basic strings in this case, as shown in Listing 9-5.

LISTING 9-5: Creating StringListAdapter

```
package com.wiley.wrox.walkkeeper;

import android.content.Context;
import android.support.wearable.view.WearableListView;
import android.view.LayoutInflater;
import android.view.ViewGroup;
import android.widget.TextView;

public class StringListAdapter extends WearableListView.Adapter {

  private String[] data;
  private LayoutInflater mLayoutInflater;

  public StringListAdapter(Context context, String[] data) {
    mLayoutInflater = LayoutInflater.from(context);
    this.data = data;
  }

  @Override
  public WearableListView.ViewHolder onCreateViewHolder(ViewGroup group, int i) {
```

```
        return new WearableListView.ViewHolder(mLayoutInflater.inflate(R.layout
            .stringlist_item, group, false));
    }

    @Override
    public void onBindViewHolder(WearableListView.ViewHolder viewHolder, int i) {
        TextView text = (TextView) viewHolder.itemView.findViewById(R.id
            .stringlist_item_text);
        text.setText(data[i]);
    }

    @Override
    public int getItemCount() {
        return data.length;
    }
}
```

You'll notice an error. We haven't created the layout for the list item row. Listing 9-6 shows the simple layout we'll use for all the WearableListView rows in this project.

LISTING 9-6: Building the list view row layout

```
<?xml version="1.0" encoding="utf-8"?>
<LinearLayout
    xmlns:android="http://schemas.android.com/apk/res/android"
    android:layout_width="match_parent"
    android:layout_height="match_parent">

    <TextView
        android:id="@+id/stringlist_item_text"
        android:layout_width="match_parent"
        android:layout_height="wrap_content"
        android:text="..."/>
</LinearLayout>
```

Instantiate StringListAdapter and connect it to WearableListView in SelectGenderActivity. In Listing 9-7, the changes in SelectGenderActivity are highlighted.

LISTING 9-7: Wrapping up SelectGenderActivity

```
package com.wiley.wrox.walkkeeper;

import android.app.Activity;
import android.os.Bundle;
import android.support.wearable.view.WatchViewStub;
import android.support.wearable.view.WearableListView;

public class SelectGenderActivity extends Activity {

    private String[] mData = new String[]{"\u2640 female", "\u2642 male"};
    private WearableListView mListView;
```

continues

LISTING 9-7 *(continued)*

```
    private StringListAdapter mAdapter;

    @Override
    protected void onCreate(Bundle savedInstanceState) {
      super.onCreate(savedInstanceState);
      setContentView(R.layout.activity_select_gender);
      final WatchViewStub stub = (WatchViewStub) findViewById(R.id.watch_view_stub);
      stub.setOnLayoutInflatedListener(new WatchViewStub.OnLayoutInflatedListener() {
        @Override
        public void onLayoutInflated(WatchViewStub stub) {
          mListView = (WearableListView) stub.findViewById(R.id.list);
          mAdapter = new StringListAdapter(SelectGenderActivity.this, mdata);
          mListView.setAdapter(mAdapter);
        }
      });
    }
  }
```

You should end up with a simple list that has two items, similar to Figure 9-2.

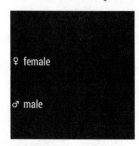

FIGURE 9-2: The select
gender list

Finally, attach the listener to `WearableListView`, and save the selected value, as shown in Listing 9-8.

LISTING 9-8: Saving the selected gender and moving to the next activity

```
package com.wiley.wrox.walkkeeper;

import android.app.Activity;
import android.content.SharedPreferences;
import android.os.Bundle;
import android.support.wearable.view.WatchViewStub;
import android.support.wearable.view.WearableListView;

public class SelectGenderActivity extends Activity {

  private String[] mData = new String[]{"\u2640 female", "\u2642 male"};
  private WearableListView mListView;
  private StringListAdapter mAdapter;

  @Override
```

```
protected void onCreate(Bundle savedInstanceState) {
  super.onCreate(savedInstanceState);
  setContentView(R.layout.activity_select_gender);
  final WatchViewStub stub = (WatchViewStub) findViewById(R.id.watch_view_stub);
  stub.setOnLayoutInflatedListener(new WatchViewStub.OnLayoutInflatedListener() {
    @Override
    public void onLayoutInflated(WatchViewStub stub) {
      mListView = (WearableListView) stub.findViewById(R.id.list);
      mAdapter = new StringListAdapter(SelectGenderActivity.this, mdata);
      mListView.setAdapter(mAdapter);
      mListView.setClickListener(new WearableListView.ClickListener() {
        @Override
        public void onClick(WearableListView.ViewHolder viewHolder) {
          String label = mdata[viewHolder.getPosition()];
          if (label.contains("female")) {
            saveGender("female");
          } else {
            saveGender("male");
          }
          openSelectWeightActivity();
        }

        @Override
        public void onTopEmptyRegionClick() {

        }
      });
    }
  });
}

private void saveGender(String gender) {
  SharedPreferences prefs = getPreferences(MODE_PRIVATE);
  SharedPreferences.Editor editor = prefs.edit();
  editor.putString("gender", gender);
  editor.apply();
}

private void openSelectWeightActivity() {
  // TODO: Start activity SelectWeightActivity
}
}
```

You'll soon create the activity for selecting a specific weight. Before you create it you can create the intent for starting that activity, as shown in Listing 9-9.

LISTING 9-9: Open the SelectWeight activity

```
private void openSelectWeightActivity() {
  Intent selectWeight = new Intent(this, SelectWeightActivity.class);
  startActivity(selectWeight);
  finish();
}
```

Selecting Weight

Create a new activity by selecting File ➤ New ➤ Activity ➤ Blank Wear Activity.

Call your new activity **SelectWeightActivity**, and uncheck the Launcher Activity check box before you click Finish.

In this activity we'll use the same setup as the previous activity, with `WearableListView` attached to `ClickListener`. We'll reuse the previously created `StringListAdapter` and layouts. Listing 9-10 shows `SelectWeightActivity` in its entirety. You'll notice we decided to go with kilograms. You can, of course, change this. Just remember to modify how you calculate the calories later.

LISTING 9-10: SelectWeightActivity

```
package com.wiley.wrox.walkkeeper;

import android.app.Activity;
import android.content.SharedPreferences;
import android.os.Bundle;
import android.support.wearable.view.WatchViewStub;
import android.support.wearable.view.WearableListView;

public class SelectWeightActivity extends Activity {

  private String[] mData = new String[]{"60", "65", "70", "75", "80", "85", "90"};
  private WearableListView mListView;
  private StringListAdapter mAdapter;

  @Override
  protected void onCreate(Bundle savedInstanceState) {
    super.onCreate(savedInstanceState);
    setContentView(R.layout.activity_select_weight);
    final WatchViewStub stub = (WatchViewStub) findViewById(R.id.watch_view_stub);
    stub.setOnLayoutInflatedListener(new WatchViewStub.OnLayoutInflatedListener() {
      @Override
      public void onLayoutInflated(WatchViewStub stub) {
        mListView = (WearableListView) stub.findViewById(R.id.list);
        mAdapter = new StringListAdapter(SelectWeightActivity.this, mdata);
        mListView.setAdapter(mAdapter);

        mListView.setClickListener(new WearableListView.ClickListener() {
          @Override
          public void onClick(WearableListView.ViewHolder viewHolder) {
            String label = mdata[viewHolder.getPosition()];
            saveWeight(Integer.parseInt(label));
            openSelectHeightActivity();
          }

          @Override
          public void onTopEmptyRegionClick() {

          }
```

```
                });
            }
        });
    }

    private void saveWeight(int weight) {
        SharedPreferences prefs = getPreferences(MODE_PRIVATE);
        SharedPreferences.Editor editor = prefs.edit();
        editor.putInt("W", weight);
        editor.apply();
    }

    private void openSelectHeightActivity() {
        // TODO: Start activity SelectHeightActivity
    }
}
```

Add `WearableListView` to the layouts, and you're done with this activity. Listing 9-11 shows the rectangular layout version; the round layout is nearly identical.

LISTING 9-11: Adding WearableListView to the Select Weight layouts

```
<?xml version="1.0" encoding="utf-8"?>
<LinearLayout
    xmlns:android="http://schemas.android.com/apk/res/android"
    xmlns:tools="http://schemas.android.com/tools"
    android:layout_width="match_parent"
    android:layout_height="match_parent"
    android:orientation="vertical"
    tools:context="com.wiley.wrox.walkkeeper.SelectWeightActivity"
    tools:deviceIds="wear_square">

    <android.support.wearable.view.WearableListView
        android:id="@+id/list"
        android:layout_width="match_parent"
        android:layout_height="match_parent"/>
</LinearLayout>
```

The finished Select Weight view should look something like Figure 9-3.

FIGURE 9-3: The finished
select weight list

To open the SelectHeight activity, which is still not created, add the intent inside openSelectHeightActivity method and call startActivity, as shown in Listing 9-12. You'll get an error but that will be quickly remedied in the following section.

LISTING 9-12: Start the SelectHeight activity

```java
private void openSelectHeightActivity() {
    Intent selectHeight = new Intent(this, SelectHeightActivity.class);
    startActivity(selectHeight);
    finish();
}
```

Selecting Height

The last setup step for the WalkKeeper app is the Select Height activity. Again, this is a list with a set number of available heights.

1. Create a new activity by selecting File ➤ New ➤ Activity ➤ Blank Wear Activity.

2. Name the new activity **SelectHeightActivity**, and unselect the Launcher Activity check box.

3. Open your new activity, and add the highlighted code shown in Listing 9-13.

LISTING 9-13: The Select Height activity

```java
package com.wiley.wrox.walkkeeper;

import android.app.Activity;
import android.content.SharedPreferences;
import android.os.Bundle;
import android.support.wearable.view.WatchViewStub;
import android.support.wearable.view.WearableListView;

public class SelectHeightActivity extends Activity {

    private String[] mData = new String[]{"160", "165", "170", "175", "180"};
    private WearableListView mListView;
    private StringListAdapter mAdapter;

    @Override
    protected void onCreate(Bundle savedInstanceState) {
        super.onCreate(savedInstanceState);
        setContentView(R.layout.activity_select_height);
        final WatchViewStub stub = (WatchViewStub) findViewById(R.id.watch_view_stub);
        stub.setOnLayoutInflatedListener(new WatchViewStub.OnLayoutInflatedListener() {
            @Override
            public void onLayoutInflated(WatchViewStub stub) {
                mListView = (WearableListView) stub.findViewById(R.id.list);
                mAdapter = new StringListAdapter(SelectHeightActivity.this, mdata);
```

```
      mListView.setAdapter(mAdapter);

      mListView.setClickListener(new WearableListView.ClickListener() {
        @Override
        public void onClick(WearableListView.ViewHolder viewHolder) {
          String label = mdata[viewHolder.getPosition()];
          saveHeight(Integer.parseInt(label));
          openWalkKeeperActivity();
        }

        @Override
        public void onTopEmptyRegionClick() {

        }
      });
    }
  });
}

private void saveHeight(int height) {
  SharedPreferences prefs = getPreferences(MODE_PRIVATE);
  SharedPreferences.Editor editor = prefs.edit();
  editor.putInt("H", height);
  editor.apply();
}

private void openWalkKeeperActivity() {
  // TODO: Open WalkKeeperActivity
}
}
```

Finally, edit the layouts for the Select Height activity as shown in Listing 9-14.

LISTING 9-14: The Select Height layouts

```
<?xml version="1.0" encoding="utf-8"?>
<LinearLayout
    xmlns:android="http://schemas.android.com/apk/res/android"
    xmlns:tools="http://schemas.android.com/tools"
    android:layout_width="match_parent"
    android:layout_height="match_parent"
    android:orientation="vertical"
    tools:context="com.wiley.wrox.walkkeeper.SelectHeightActivity"
    tools:deviceIds="wear_square">

  <android.support.wearable.view.WearableListView
      android:id="@+id/list"
      android:layout_width="match_parent"
      android:layout_height="match_parent"/>
</LinearLayout>
```

The finished Select Height activity should look like Figure 9-4.

FIGURE 9-4: Select
Height activity

When the user is done selecting all of the preferences, it's time to start the WalkKeeper activity which will present the active view to the user. Listing 9-15 shows how to create this intent.

LISTING 9-15: Start the WalkKeeper activity

```
private void openWalkKeeperActivity() {
    Intent walkKeeper = new Intent(this, WalkKeeperActivity.class);
    startActivity(walkKeeper);
    finish();
}
```

The WalkKeeper Activity

The final and most important piece of the puzzle is the WalkKeeper activity, where all logic for calculating steps taken and calories burned happens. This is also where we display the live data to the user.

1. Start by creating a new activity. Select File ➤ New ➤ Activity ➤ Blank Wear Activity.

2. Name your activity **WalkKeeperActivity**, and uncheck the Launcher Activity check box.

Building the User Interface

On the main WalkKeeper user interface, we'll display both the total number of steps taken during this session and the calories burned during the stroll. Listing 9-16 shows the entire layout with all the TextViews we'll use.

LISTING 9-16: The WalkKeeper user interface

```
<?xml version="1.0" encoding="utf-8"?>
<LinearLayout
    xmlns:android="http://schemas.android.com/apk/res/android"
    xmlns:tools="http://schemas.android.com/tools"
    android:layout_width="match_parent"
```

```
            android:layout_height="match_parent"
            android:orientation="vertical"
            tools:context="com.wiley.wrox.walkkeeper.WalkKeeperActivity"
            tools:deviceIds="wear_square">

    <LinearLayout
        android:layout_width="match_parent"
        android:layout_height="match_parent"
        android:layout_weight="1"
        android:orientation="vertical">

        <TextView
            android:id="@+id/title_steps"
            android:layout_width="wrap_content"
            android:layout_height="wrap_content"
            android:text="Steps taken:"
            android:textAppearance="?android:attr/textAppearanceLarge"/>

        <TextView
            android:id="@+id/text_steps"
            android:layout_width="wrap_content"
            android:layout_height="wrap_content"
            android:text="0"
            android:textAppearance="?android:attr/textAppearanceMedium"/>
    </LinearLayout>

    <LinearLayout
        android:layout_width="match_parent"
        android:layout_height="match_parent"
        android:layout_weight="1"
        android:orientation="vertical">

        <TextView
            android:id="@+id/title_calories"
            android:layout_width="wrap_content"
            android:layout_height="wrap_content"
            android:text="Calories burned"
            android:textAppearance="?android:attr/textAppearanceLarge"/>

        <TextView
            android:id="@+id/text_calories"
            android:layout_width="wrap_content"
            android:layout_height="wrap_content"
            android:text="0"
            android:textAppearance="?android:attr/textAppearanceMedium"/>
    </LinearLayout>
</LinearLayout>
```

Connecting the User Interface

We've used standard activities so far in the app. However, for this activity I want to allow the user to touch to close the app, as shown in Figure 9-5. Because of this I will let the `WalkKeeperActivity` extend `InsetActivity` rather than `Activity`. This will also make us load views in a different way—instead of using a `WatchViewStub` we'll rely on the `onReadyForContent()` life-cycle method.

FIGURE 9-5: The touch-
to-close option

Open WalkKeeperActivity.java and extend `InsetActivity`, as shown in Listing 9-17.

LISTING 9-17: Extending InsetActivity

```java
package com.wiley.wrox.walkkeeper;

import android.os.Bundle;
import android.support.wearable.activity.InsetActivity;

public class WalkKeeperActivity extends InsetActivity {

  @Override
  protected void onCreate(Bundle savedInstanceState) {
    super.onCreate(savedInstanceState);
  }

  @Override
  public void onReadyForContent() {
    if (!isRound()) {
      setContentView(R.layout.rect_activity_walk_keeper);
    } else {
      setContentView(R.layout.round_activity_walk_keeper);
    }
  }
}
```

Load the user interface widgets into variables to enable changing them live. See Listing 9-18 for hints.

LISTING 9-18: Loading the user interface

```java
package com.wiley.wrox.walkkeeper;

import android.os.Bundle;
import android.support.wearable.activity.InsetActivity;
import android.widget.TextView;

public class WalkKeeperActivity extends InsetActivity {

  private TextView stepsCount, caloriesCount;
```

```
        @Override
        protected void onCreate(Bundle savedInstanceState) {
          super.onCreate(savedInstanceState);
        }

        @Override
        public void onReadyForContent() {
          if (!isRound()) {
            setContentView(R.layout.rect_activity_walk_keeper);
          } else {
            setContentView(R.layout.round_activity_walk_keeper);
          }
          stepsCount = (TextView) findViewById(R.id.text_steps);
          caloriesCount = (TextView) findViewById(R.id.text_calories);
        }
      }
```

Getting the Stored Settings

When we're done with the user interface, we can move on to loading the previous saved user data—gender, weight, and height. See Listing 9-19 for details.

LISTING 9-19: Loading the stored user data

```
package com.wiley.wrox.walkkeeper;

import android.content.SharedPreferences;
import android.os.Bundle;
import android.support.wearable.activity.InsetActivity;
import android.widget.TextView;

public class WalkKeeperActivity extends InsetActivity {

  private TextView stepsCount, caloriesCount;

  private String gender;
  private int W, H;

  @Override
  protected void onCreate(Bundle savedInstanceState) {
    super.onCreate(savedInstanceState);
    SharedPreferences prefs = getPreferences(MODE_PRIVATE);
    gender = prefs.getString("gender", "female");
    W = prefs.getInt("W", 80);
    H = prefs.getInt("H", 180);
  }

  @Override
  public void onReadyForContent() {
    if (!isRound()) {
      setContentView(R.layout.rect_activity_walk_keeper);
    } else {
      setContentView(R.layout.round_activity_walk_keeper);
```

continues

LISTING 9-19 *(continued)*

```
    }
    stepsCount = (TextView) findViewById(R.id.text_steps);
    caloriesCount = (TextView) findViewById(R.id.text_calories);
  }


}
```

Reading the Sensor Data

This example uses the Step Detector sensor because we want many quick readings for testing. We could use the Step Counter sensor as well, but I'll leave that for you to implement if you want a more accurate reading. Add the `uses-feature` element for the Step Detector sensor as shown in Listing 9-20.

LISTING 9-20: Adding uses-feature for the Step Detector sensor

```xml
<?xml version="1.0" encoding="utf-8"?>
<manifest
  package="com.wiley.wrox.walkkeeper"
  xmlns:android="http://schemas.android.com/apk/res/android">

  <uses-feature android:name="android.hardware.type.watch"/>
  <uses-feature android:name="android.hardware.sensor.stepdetector"/>

  <application
    android:allowBackup="true"
    android:icon="@drawable/ic_launcher"
    android:label="@string/app_name"
    android:theme="@android:style/Theme.DeviceDefault">

    <activity
      android:name=".SelectGenderActivity"
      android:label="@string/app_name">
      <intent-filter>
        <action android:name="android.intent.action.MAIN"/>
        <category android:name="android.intent.category.LAUNCHER"/>
      </intent-filter>
    </activity>

    <activity
      android:name=".SelectWeightActivity"
      android:label="@string/title_activity_select_weight">
    </activity>

    <activity
      android:name=".SelectHeightActivity"
      android:label="@string/title_activity_select_height">
    </activity>

    <activity
      android:name=".WalkKeeperActivity"
```

```
              android:label="@string/title_activity_walk_keeper">
        </activity>
    </application>
</manifest>
```

Open `WalkKeeperActivity` and declare `SensorManager` and `Sensor` variables. Then load them and attach a listener, as shown in highlights in Listing 9-21.

LISTING 9-21: Attaching the sensor to WalkKeeperActivity

```java
package com.wiley.wrox.walkkeeper;

import android.content.SharedPreferences;
import android.hardware.Sensor;
import android.hardware.SensorEvent;
import android.hardware.SensorEventListener;
import android.hardware.SensorManager;
import android.os.Bundle;
import android.support.wearable.activity.InsetActivity;
import android.widget.TextView;

public class WalkKeeperActivity extends InsetActivity {

  private TextView stepsCount, caloriesCount;

  private String gender;
  private int W, H;

  private SensorManager mSensorManager;
  private Sensor mSensor;
  private int S;

  @Override
  protected void onCreate(Bundle savedInstanceState) {
    super.onCreate(savedInstanceState);
    SharedPreferences prefs = getPreferences(MODE_PRIVATE);
    gender = prefs.getString("gender", "female");
    W = prefs.getInt("W", 80);
    H = prefs.getInt("H", 180);

    mSensorManager = (SensorManager) getSystemService(SENSOR_SERVICE);
    mSensor = mSensorManager.getDefaultSensor(Sensor.TYPE_STEP_DETECTOR);
  }

  @Override
  protected void onResume() {
    super.onResume();
    mSensorManager.registerListener(mSensorEventListener, mSensor, 1000);
  }

  @Override
  protected void onPause() {
    super.onPause();
```

continues

LISTING 9-21 *(continued)*

```
    mSensorManager.unregisterListener(mSensorEventListener);
  }

  @Override
  public void onReadyForContent() {
    if (!isRound()) {
      setContentView(R.layout.rect_activity_walk_keeper);
    } else {
      setContentView(R.layout.round_activity_walk_keeper);
    }
    stepsCount = (TextView) findViewById(R.id.text_steps);
    caloriesCount = (TextView) findViewById(R.id.text_calories);
  }

  private SensorEventListener mSensorEventListener = new SensorEventListener() {
    @Override
    public void onSensorChanged(SensorEvent sensorEvent) {
      S += (int) sensorEvent.values[0];
    }

    @Override
    public void onAccuracyChanged(Sensor sensor, int i) {
    }
  };

}
```

Now we're getting the sensor values, which means we're almost at the finish line. We just need to calculate the calories and then update the user interface.

Calculating and Updating the User Interface

Start by calculating the calories, as shown in Listing 9-22. Note that this example uses the metric system. You can use the formula from equation 3 in the earlier section "Calculating Calories."

LISTING 9-22: Calculating the calories from the number of steps

```
package com.wiley.wrox.walkkeeper;

import android.content.SharedPreferences;
import android.hardware.Sensor;
import android.hardware.SensorEvent;
import android.hardware.SensorEventListener;
import android.hardware.SensorManager;
import android.os.Bundle;
import android.support.wearable.activity.InsetActivity;
import android.widget.TextView;

public class WalkKeeperActivity extends InsetActivity {

  private static final double STRIDE_FACTOR_FEMALE = 0.413;
```

```java
private static final double STRIDE_FACTOR_MALE = 0.415;

private TextView stepsCount, caloriesCount;

private String gender;
private int W, H;

private SensorManager mSensorManager;
private Sensor mSensor;
private int S;
private double TCB;

@Override
protected void onCreate(Bundle savedInstanceState) {
  super.onCreate(savedInstanceState);
  SharedPreferences prefs = getPreferences(MODE_PRIVATE);
  gender = prefs.getString("gender", "male");
  W = prefs.getInt("W", 80);
  H = prefs.getInt("H", 180);

  mSensorManager = (SensorManager) getSystemService(SENSOR_SERVICE);
  mSensor = mSensorManager.getDefaultSensor(Sensor.TYPE_STEP_DETECTOR);
}

@Override
protected void onResume() {
  super.onResume();
  mSensorManager.registerListener(mSensorEventListener, mSensor, 1000);
}

@Override
protected void onPause() {
  super.onPause();
  mSensorManager.unregisterListener(mSensorEventListener);
}

@Override
public void onReadyForContent() {
  if (!isRound()) {
    setContentView(R.layout.rect_activity_walk_keeper);
  } else {
    setContentView(R.layout.round_activity_walk_keeper);
  }
  stepsCount = (TextView) findViewById(R.id.text_steps);
  caloriesCount = (TextView) findViewById(R.id.text_calories);
}

private SensorEventListener mSensorEventListener = new SensorEventListener() {
  @Override
  public void onSensorChanged(SensorEvent sensorEvent) {
    S += (int) sensorEvent.values[0];
    TCB = getCalories();
    updateUserInterface();
```

continues

LISTING 9-22 *(continued)*

```
      }

      @Override
      public void onAccuracyChanged(Sensor sensor, int i) {
      }
  };

  private double getCalories() {
    double CBD = W * 2.02;
    double D = 0;
    if (gender.equals("female")) {
      D = H * STRIDE_FACTOR_FEMALE * S * 0.00001;
    }else{
      D = H * STRIDE_FACTOR_MALE * S * 0.00001;
    }
    return CBD * D;
  }

  private void updateUserInterface(){
    if( stepsCount != null ){
      stepsCount.setText(Integer.toString(S));
    }
    if( caloriesCount != null ){
      caloriesCount.setText(Double.toString(TCB));
    }
  }
}
```

Keeping the Activity Open

As you know, Android Wear automatically closes activities after a short period. But we'll keep the activity running until the user actively closes it by touching the screen. This lets us avoid having to store any state in the activity—something you can explore on your own.

Keeping the activity open in this way will drain significantly more battery than normal. A more correct way of solving this problem would be using a Service that collects data and does the calculations in the background. This way the Activity can be destroyed without losing any data.

There are multiple ways to keep the screen awake. We'll apply a special flag during startup of the WalkKeeper activity, as shown in Listing 9-23.

LISTING 9-23: Keeping the screen awake

```
package com.wiley.wrox.walkkeeper;

import android.content.SharedPreferences;
import android.hardware.Sensor;
import android.hardware.SensorEvent;
import android.hardware.SensorEventListener;
import android.hardware.SensorManager;
```

```java
import android.os.Bundle;
import android.support.wearable.activity.InsetActivity;
import android.view.WindowManager;
import android.widget.TextView;

public class WalkKeeperActivity extends InsetActivity {
  private static final double STRIDE_FACTOR_FEMALE = 0.413;
  private static final double STRIDE_FACTOR_MALE = 0.415;

  private TextView stepsCount, caloriesCount;

  private String gender;
  private int W, H;

  private SensorManager mSensorManager;
  private Sensor mSensor;
  private int S;
  private double TCB;

  @Override
  protected void onCreate(Bundle savedInstanceState) {
    super.onCreate(savedInstanceState);
    SharedPreferences prefs = getPreferences(MODE_PRIVATE);
    gender = prefs.getString("gender", "male");
    W = prefs.getInt("W", 80);
    H = prefs.getInt("H", 180);

    mSensorManager = (SensorManager) getSystemService(SENSOR_SERVICE);
    mSensor = mSensorManager.getDefaultSensor(Sensor.TYPE_STEP_DETECTOR);
  }

  @Override
  protected void onResume() {
    super.onResume();
    mSensorManager.registerListener(mSensorEventListener, mSensor, 1000);
  }

  @Override
  protected void onPause() {
    super.onPause();
    mSensorManager.unregisterListener(mSensorEventListener);
  }

  @Override
  public void onReadyForContent() {
    if (!isRound()) {
      setContentView(R.layout.rect_activity_walk_keeper);
    } else {
      setContentView(R.layout.round_activity_walk_keeper);
    }

    getWindow().addFlags(WindowManager.LayoutParams.FLAG_KEEP_SCREEN_ON);

    stepsCount = (TextView) findViewById(R.id.text_steps);
```

continues

LISTING 9-23 *(continued)*

```java
        caloriesCount = (TextView) findViewById(R.id.text_calories);
    }

    private SensorEventListener mSensorEventListener = new SensorEventListener() {
      @Override
      public void onSensorChanged(SensorEvent sensorEvent) {
        S += (int) sensorEvent.values[0];
        TCB = getCalories();
        upateUserInterface();
      }

      @Override
      public void onAccuracyChanged(Sensor sensor, int i) {
      }
    };

    private double getCalories() {
      double CPD = W * 2.02;
      double D = 0;
      if (gender.equals("female")) {
        D = H * STRIDE_FACTOR_FEMALE * S * 0.00001;
      }else{
        D = H * STRIDE_FACTOR_MALE * S * 0.00001;
      }
      return CPD * D;
    }

    private void upateUserInterface(){
      if( stepsCount != null ){
        stepsCount.setText(Integer.toString(S));
      }
      if( caloriesCount != null ){
        caloriesCount.setText(Double.toString(TCB));
      }
    }

}
```

The finished WalkKeeper app should look something like Figure 9-6.

FIGURE 9-6: The finished
WalkKeeper app

This is a simple demonstration of what Android Wear and the new hardware sensors available in Kit Kat can do. There are still a million things you can, and should, do with this app before it can be distributed on Google Play.

IMPROVEMENTS

Here are some things you should consider improving in this project that we haven't discussed in this chapter:

- ➤ Move the data collection and calculations to a Service.

- ➤ Connect the app to Google Fit.

- ➤ Design a more attractive user interface that is specifically made for Wear. Remember the rule of thumb with Wear user interfaces: They should be glanceable.

- ➤ Another thing you could improve with this app are the transitions between activities.

- ➤ Another obvious improvement is asking the user for his or her weight only once, and then after that automatically calculating the most probable weight according to his or her activity history.

- ➤ Last, but not least, is improving the sensor readings. You could consider not only changing the sensors but including more sensors to expand the app's functionality.

The final thing you should do with this app is create the companion mobile app. This task is not listed in the improvements because it's not so much an improvement as it is a requirement to publish on Google Play. You need the companion app to distribute the app!

SUMMARY

In this chapter you've seen examples of use for some of the new user interface widgets introduced in Android Wear. You also were introduced to using passive sensors in Wear apps.

The next chapter deals with active use of sensors to create interesting interactions with your Wear device.

10

Smartwatch as Input

WHAT'S IN THIS CHAPTER?

➤ Using Wear as a game controller

➤ Using sensors on Android Wear

➤ Gesture detection with accelerometers

➤ Sending data between devices

WROX.COM CODE DOWNLOADS FOR THIS CHAPTER

The code downloads for this chapter are found at www.wrox.com/go/androidwearables on the Download Code tab. The code is in the Chapter 10 download and the files are individually named according to the listing numbers noted throughout the chapter.

ANDROID WEAR AS A GAME CONTROLLER

Chapter 9 reviewed how to use sensors on Android Wear when building a basic Activity Tracker application. The Activity Tracker was only running on Android Wear and was not connected to your phone in any way. This is poor design because Google requires you to at least have a host app when publishing on Google Play.

In this chapter we'll remedy this problem by building a simple dice game—without any dice!—running on both devices. We will use Android Wear to create the virtual die that will be thrown on the mobile device. We will read its accelerometer sensor and translate its movements to the number of distinct shake gestures performed.

The value of shake gestures will then be translated into a random value on a selected die and displayed on your game board.

A Note on Sensors

Android devices have a multitude of sensors available. Even the small Android Wear device has as many as 15 or even more, as shown in Table 10-1. Some of them are compound or composite sensors. This means that we often have more than one choice for how to solve a sensor-based problem. This chapter presents just one solution to the virtual dice problem.

TABLE 10-1: Sensors Available on the LG G Watch

NAME	TYPE	DESCRIPTION
STMicro 3-axis Tilt Sensor	Software	
MPL Gyroscope	Hardware	
MPL Raw Gyroscope	Hardware	
MPL Accelerometer	Hardware	An accelerometer sensor that includes the gravity force.
MPL Magnetic Field	Hardware	
MPL Raw Magnetic Field	Hardware	
MPL Orientation	Software	An older-style sensor that has been deprecated and is on its way out of the Android system. You should use the Rotation Vector instead.
MPL Rotation Vector	Software	Gives a rotational unit vector based on the East-North-Up coordinates.
MPL Game Rotation Vector	Software	Similar to the Rotation Vector, except that it uses different underlying hardware. This also means that the sensors report different values.
MPL Linear Acceleration	Software	An accelerometer that has the gravity already excluded.
MPL Gravity	Software	Reports the gravity vector in the device's coordinate system. Should be identical to the raw accelerometer values when the device is resting.
MPL Signification Motion	Software	A composite sensor that allows the device to fall asleep while the sensor is still working, which is very different from other sensors. This sensor is often used to listen for when the user starts to walk, run, bike, or something else.
MPL Step Detector	Hardware/software	Fires a single event for every detected step the user takes while the sensor is active. Chapter 9 covered this sensor.
MPL Step Counter	Hardware/software	Keeps track of the total number of steps the user has taken since the device was started. It resets the number of steps when the device is turned off or rebooted.
MPL Geomagnetic Rotation Vector	Software	Also called a magnetometer and is very similar to the rotation vector sensor. However, where the rotation vector uses a gyroscope, this uses the magnetometer. It reports the same set of values as the rotation vector.

Detecting Gestures

To understand basic gesture detection with accelerometers, first we need to review the data the accelerometer produces. Looking at graphs helps us understand what the motion looks like to the computer and how values are translated over time. Figure 10-1 shows a graph of a simple shake gesture with a Wear device attached to your wrist.

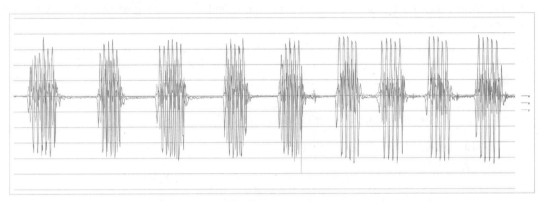

FIGURE 10-1: The shake gesture as the computer sees it

Notice how the single shake motion in one direction has two almost-equal forces—acceleration and deceleration. The objective is to detect these pairs of motions to create a single shake movement.

Creating more-complex gestures may even require "training" your device to recognize the gesture. But this topic is beyond the scope of this chapter, so we'll leave it to you to explore on your own.

BUILDING THE DICE GAME

In this chapter we'll build a project using the accelerometer sensor (TYPE_ACCELEROMETER) to detect shake gestures. We define a shake gesture as a rapid set of motions that change direction. You can think of the smartwatch as a simple, safe, miniature version of the Wiimote. There's no chance you'll injure your spouse while playing tennis with the Wear device if you attach it to your wrist properly.

Creating the Project

Begin by creating the project for our game. Enter **DiceGame** as the Application name, and let the Company Domain be **wrox.wiley.com**. Select both the Phone and Tablet and the Wear platforms for this app; we'll use the smartwatch as the virtual die and the phone as the game board. Create both the activities. Call the Phone activity **MyPhoneActivity** and the Wear activity **MyWearActivity**. Click Finish to create the project.

Designing a User Interface

A game is a complex structure. Even a seemingly simple game such as Yahtzee requires a lot of logic to handle all the possible outcomes. We won't be doing any of that. We'll focus solely on the game's interactions—the dice throw. If you want to build a full game with all the bells and whistles, we recommend that you visit any of the excellent game-building tutorial websites. You'll find plenty of material to dig through!

Android Wear GUI

Our interface is simple. On the Wear side we'll use a `CircledImageView` as a progress indicator for the dice throw, showing that a dice throw is in progress and also showing when we'll force the die to be thrown.

When the die has been thrown, we'll let the user know that a successful throw has been made. Listing 10-1 shows our rectangular layout for Wear. Notice that we've added the XML namespace so that we can easily set the required attributes.

LISTING 10-1: The Wear layout, rect format

```xml
<?xml version="1.0" encoding="utf-8"?>
<LinearLayout
    xmlns:android="http://schemas.android.com/apk/res/android"
    xmlns:tools="http://schemas.android.com/tools"
    xmlns:wear="http://schemas.android.com/apk/res-auto"
    android:layout_width="match_parent"
    android:layout_height="match_parent"
    android:background="@color/white"
    android:orientation="vertical"
    tools:context=".MyWearActivity"
    tools:deviceIds="wear_square">

  <android.support.wearable.view.CircledImageView
    android:id="@+id/progress"
    android:layout_width="match_parent"
    android:layout_height="match_parent"
    wear:circle_border_color="#33CCFF"
    wear:circle_border_width="15dp"
    wear:circle_color="@color/white"
    wear:circle_radius="80dp"
    />

</LinearLayout>
```

We'll use a `CountDownTimer` to both animate the progress indicator on the `CircledImageView` and provide a fail-safe exit for the dice throw. A player shouldn't be allowed to shake the dice for an eternity! Listing 10-2 highlights the timer.

LISTING 10-2: Adding the progress animation

```java
package com.wiley.wrox.dicegame;

import android.app.Activity;
import android.os.Bundle;
import android.os.CountDownTimer;
```

```java
import android.support.wearable.view.CircledImageView;
import android.support.wearable.view.WatchViewStub;

public class MyWearActivity extends Activity {

  private static final int MAX_SHAKE_TIME = 1000;
  private static final int COUNTDOWN_INTERVAL = 100;

  private CircledImageView mCircledImageView;

  private CountDownTimer mCountDownTimer;

  @Override
  protected void onCreate(Bundle savedInstanceState) {
    super.onCreate(savedInstanceState);
    setContentView(R.layout.activity_my_wear);
    final WatchViewStub stub = (WatchViewStub) findViewById(R.id.watch_view_stub);
    stub.setOnLayoutInflatedListener(new WatchViewStub.OnLayoutInflatedListener() {
      @Override
      public void onLayoutInflated(WatchViewStub stub) {
        mCircledImageView = (CircledImageView) stub.findViewById(R.id.progress);
        startTimer(); // Test the timer
      }
    });

  }

  private void startTimer() {
    if (mCountDownTimer != null)
      mCountDownTimer.cancel();

    mCountDownTimer = new CountDownTimer(MAX_SHAKE_TIME, COUNTDOWN_INTERVAL) {
      @Override
      public void onTick(long millisLeft) {
        float progress = (float) millisLeft/MAX_SHAKE_TIME;
        mCircledImageView.setProgress(progress);
      }

      @Override
      public void onFinish() {
        mCircledImageView.setProgress(1.0f);
      }
    };

    mCountDownTimer.start();
  }
}
```

That concludes the Wear UI. Let's move on to the mobile's UI, which is even simpler.

Mobile GUI

On the mobile side of things is an even more basic interface—a TextView displaying the resulting throw. That's it! See Listing 10-3 for details.

LISTING 10-3: The mobile layout

```xml
<RelativeLayout
    xmlns:android="http://schemas.android.com/apk/res/android"
    xmlns:tools="http://schemas.android.com/tools"
    android:layout_width="match_parent"
    android:layout_height="match_parent"
    android:paddingBottom="@dimen/activity_vertical_margin"
    android:paddingLeft="@dimen/activity_horizontal_margin"
    android:paddingRight="@dimen/activity_horizontal_margin"
    android:paddingTop="@dimen/activity_vertical_margin"
    tools:context=".MyPhoneActivity">

    <TextView
      android:layout_width="wrap_content"
      android:layout_height="wrap_content"
      android:layout_alignParentTop="true"
      android:layout_centerHorizontal="true"
      android:layout_marginTop="10dp"
      android:text="@string/app_name"
      android:textSize="40sp"/>

    <TextView
      android:id="@+id/result"
      android:layout_width="wrap_content"
      android:layout_height="wrap_content"
      android:layout_centerInParent="true"
      android:text="0"
      android:textSize="80sp"/>

</RelativeLayout>
```

Before moving on to the application logic, be sure to hook up the UI widgets in the activity, as shown in Listing 10-4.

LISTING 10-4: Connecting the Mobile UI

```java
package com.wiley.wrox.dicegame;

import android.app.Activity;
import android.os.Bundle;
import android.widget.TextView;

public class MyPhoneActivity extends Activity {

    TextView mResult;

    @Override
    protected void onCreate(Bundle savedInstanceState) {
        super.onCreate(savedInstanceState);
```

```
    setContentView(R.layout.activity_my_phone);

    mResult = (TextView) findViewById(R.id.result);
  }

  private void setDiceValue(int value) {
    mResult.setText(Integer.toString(value));
  }
}
```

Accessing Sensors

To build this project you'll use a library called Seismic, which is made by a company called Square. The beauty of this library is that it's so simple to use in comparison to building your own shake-detection algorithm.

To include this library, add the dependency in Listing 10-5 to your Wear gradle file and then sync it.

LISTING 10-5: Add the Seismic dependency to your gradle file

```
dependencies {
  compile fileTree(dir: 'libs', include: ['*.jar'])
  compile 'com.google.android.support:wearable:+'
  compile 'com.google.android.gms:play-services-wearable:+'
  compile 'com.squareup:seismic:1.0.0'
}
```

Working with Seismic is as easy as creating an instance of ShakeListener found in the Seismic library and then passing your SensorManager to your ShakeListener. The hearShake method will be called every time a shake is registered. In Seismic, a shake is registered when more than 75% of the samples taken in the past 0.5 seconds are accelerating. This is shown in Listing 10-6.

LISTING 10-6: Fetching the sensor and attaching ShakeListener to it

```
package com.wiley.wrox.dicegame;

import android.app.Activity;
import android.hardware.SensorManager;
import com.squareup.seismic.ShakeDetector;
import android.os.Bundle;
import android.os.CountDownTimer;
import android.support.wearable.view.CircledImageView;
import android.support.wearable.view.WatchViewStub;

public class MyWearActivity extends Activity implements ShakeDetector
    .Listener {

  private static final int MAX_SHAKE_TIME = 1000;
```

continues

LISTING 10-6 *(continued)*

```java
private static final int COUNTDOWN_INTERVAL = 100;
private CircledImageView mCircledImageView;

private CountDownTimer mCountDownTimer;

private SensorManager mSensorManager;
private ShakeDetector mShakeDetector;

@Override
protected void onCreate(Bundle savedInstanceState) {
  super.onCreate(savedInstanceState);
  setContentView(R.layout.activity_my);

  mSensorManager = (SensorManager) getSystemService(SENSOR_SERVICE);
  mShakeDetector = new ShakeDetector(this);

  final WatchViewStub stub = (WatchViewStub) findViewById(R.id.watch_view_stub);
  stub.setOnLayoutInflatedListener(new WatchViewStub.OnLayoutInflatedListener() {
    @Override
    public void onLayoutInflated(WatchViewStub stub) {
      mCircledImageView = (CircledImageView) stub.findViewById(R.id.progress);
    }
  });
}

@Override
protected void onResume() {
  super.onResume();
  mShakeDetector.start(mSensorManager);
}

@Override
protected void onPause() {
  super.onPause();
  mShakeDetector.stop();
}

private void startTimer() {
  if (mCountDownTimer != null)
    mCountDownTimer.cancel();

  mCountDownTimer = new CountDownTimer(MAX_SHAKE_TIME, COUNTDOWN_INTERVAL) {
    @Override
    public void onTick(long millisLeft) {
      float progress = (float) millisLeft / MAX_SHAKE_TIME;
      mCircledImageView.setProgress(progress);
    }

    @Override
    public void onFinish() {
```

```
        mCircledImageView.setProgress(0.0f);

        // TODO: Generate die value
      }
    };

    mCountDownTimer.start();
  }

  @Override
  public void hearShake() {
    startTimer();
  }
}
```

At this point we have a working shake detector on our wrist. Before we can send anything to our game board—the mobile phone—we need to read the die value from our virtual dice.

Generating the Die Value

In this example we'll keep the die value generation simple. A basic random function multiplied with the maximum value of our standard six-sided die will suffice. Listing 10-7 shows how we generate basic random die values.

LISTING 10-7: Generating a random die value

```
package com.wiley.wrox.dicegame;

import android.app.Activity;
import android.hardware.SensorManager;
import com.squareup.seismic.ShakeDetector;
import android.os.Bundle;
import android.os.CountDownTimer;
import android.support.wearable.view.CircledImageView;
import android.support.wearable.view.WatchViewStub;

import java.util.Random;

public class MyWearActivity extends Activity implements ShakeDetector.Listener {

    ...

    private Random mRandom = new Random();

    private void startTimer() {
      if (mCountDownTimer != null)
        mCountDownTimer.cancel();

      mCountDownTimer = new CountDownTimer(MAX_SHAKE_TIME, COUNTDOWN_INTERVAL) {
```

continues

LISTING 10-7 *(continued)*

```
      @Override
      public void onTick(long millisLeft) {
        float progress = (float) millisLeft / MAX_SHAKE_TIME;
        mCircledImageView.setProgress(progress);
      }

      @Override
      public void onFinish() {
        mCircledImageView.setProgress(0.0f);

        int value = generateDieValue(6);
      }
    };

    mCountDownTimer.start();
  }

  @Override
  public void hearShake() {
    startTimer();
  }

  private int generateDieValue(int sides) {
    return mRandom.nextInt(sides) + 1;
  }
}
```

Connecting to Mobile

It's time to turn our focus to the game board. When the board is set up and ready to receive values, we need to set up the connection between it and our game control—the Wear device.

Just like we did in Chapter 7, we'll use Google Services to establish a simple data connection between our mobile and Wear devices. The connection will allow us to send simple data between the two devices.

The Mobile Connection

Open MyPhoneActivity.java and add `GoogleApiClient`, as shown in Listing 10-8.

LISTING 10-8: Adding GoogleApiClient to the mobile activity

```
package com.wiley.wrox.dicegame;

import android.app.Activity;
import android.os.Bundle;
import android.widget.TextView;

import com.google.android.gms.common.ConnectionResult;
```

```java
import com.google.android.gms.common.api.GoogleApiClient;
import com.google.android.gms.wearable.MessageApi;
import com.google.android.gms.wearable.MessageEvent;
import com.google.android.gms.wearable.Wearable;

import java.nio.ByteBuffer;


public class MyPhoneActivity extends Activity {

  TextView result;

  GoogleApiClient mGoogleApiClient;

  @Override
  protected void onCreate(Bundle savedInstanceState) {
    super.onCreate(savedInstanceState);
    setContentView(R.layout.activity_my_phone);

    result = (TextView) findViewById(R.id.result);

    mGoogleApiClient = new GoogleApiClient.Builder(this)
        .addApi(Wearable.API)
        .addConnectionCallbacks(mConnectionCallbacks)
        .build();

    mGoogleApiClient.connect();
  }

  private void setDiceValue(int value) {
    result.setText(Integer.toString(value));
  }

  GoogleApiClient.ConnectionCallbacks mConnectionCallbacks = new
      GoogleApiClient.ConnectionCallbacks() {
        @Override
        public void onConnected(Bundle bundle) {
          Wearable.MessageApi.addListener(mGoogleApiClient, mMessageListener);
        }

        @Override
        public void onConnectionSuspended(int i) {
        }
      };

  MessageApi.MessageListener mMessageListener = new MessageApi.MessageListener() {
    @Override
    public void onMessageReceived(MessageEvent messageEvent) {
      if( messageEvent.getPath().equals("/dicegame")) {
        ByteBuffer byteBuffer = ByteBuffer.wrap(messageEvent.getData());
        final int value = byteBuffer.getInt();

        runOnUiThread(new Runnable() {
          @Override
```

continues

LISTING 10-8 *(continued)*

```
        public void run() {
          setDiceValue(value);
        }
      });
    }
  }
};
}
```

INTEGERS AND BYTE ARRAYS

In Java, the standard integer has 32 bits. Because a byte consists of 8 bits, the integer actually has 4 bytes. This means that you need to translate the integer into a byte array before sending it over any data connection, which usually accepts only bytes or byte arrays.

The Wear Connection

The final part of this connection is the Wear device. Listing 10-9 shows how to create the connection on the Wear end and also how to send integers over the Google Services connection by converting them to byte arrays and then sending them as data.

LISTING 10-9: Creating GoogleApiClient on Wear

```
package com.wiley.wrox.dicegame;

import android.app.Activity;
import android.hardware.SensorManager;
import android.os.Bundle;
import android.os.CountDownTimer;
import android.support.wearable.view.CircledImageView;
import android.support.wearable.view.WatchViewStub;

import com.google.android.gms.common.api.GoogleApiClient;
import com.google.android.gms.wearable.Node;
import com.google.android.gms.wearable.NodeApi;
import com.google.android.gms.wearable.Wearable;

import java.nio.ByteBuffer;
import java.util.List;
import java.util.Random;

public class MyWearActivity extends Activity implements ShakeDetector.Listener {

  private static final int MAX_SHAKE_TIME = 1000;
  private static final int COUNTDOWN_INTERVAL = 100;
```

```java
private CircledImageView mCircledImageView;

private CountDownTimer mCountDownTimer;

private SensorManager mSensorManager;
private ShakeDetector mShakeDetector;

private Random mRandom = new Random();

private GoogleApiClient mGoogleApiClient;
private Node mNode;

@Override
protected void onCreate(Bundle savedInstanceState) {
  super.onCreate(savedInstanceState);
  setContentView(R.layout.activity_my);

  mSensorManager = (SensorManager) getSystemService(SENSOR_SERVICE);

  final WatchViewStub stub = (WatchViewStub) findViewById(R.id.watch_view_stub);
  stub.setOnLayoutInflatedListener(new WatchViewStub.OnLayoutInflatedListener() {
    @Override
    public void onLayoutInflated(WatchViewStub stub) {
      mCircledImageView = (CircledImageView) stub.findViewById(R.id.progress);
    }
  });

  mGoogleApiClient = new GoogleApiClient.Builder(this)
      .addApi(Wearable.API)
      .addConnectionCallbacks(mConnectionCallbacks)
      .build();

  mGoogleApiClient.connect();
}

@Override
protected void onResume() {
  super.onResume();
  mShakeDetector.start(mSensorManager);
}

@Override
protected void onPause() {
  super.onPause();
  mShakeDetector.stop();
}

private void startTimer() {
  if (mCountDownTimer != null)
    mCountDownTimer.cancel();

  mCountDownTimer = new CountDownTimer(MAX_SHAKE_TIME, COUNTDOWN_INTERVAL) {
    @Override
    public void onTick(long millisLeft) {
```

continues

LISTING 10-9 *(continued)*

```
      float progress = (float) millisLeft / MAX_SHAKE_TIME;
      mCircledImageView.setProgress(progress);
    }

    @Override
    public void onFinish() {
      mCircledImageView.setProgress(0.0f);

      int value = generateDieValue(6);

      sendToPhone(value);
    }
  };

  mCountDownTimer.start();
}

@Override
public void hearShake() {
  startTimer();
}

private int generateDieValue(int sides) {
  return mRandom.nextInt(sides) + 1;
}

GoogleApiClient.ConnectionCallbacks mConnectionCallbacks = new GoogleApiClient
    .ConnectionCallbacks() {
  @Override
  public void onConnected(Bundle bundle) {
    new Thread(new Runnable() {
      @Override
      public void run() {
        NodeApi.GetConnectedNodesResult result = Wearable.NodeApi
            .getConnectedNodes(mGoogleApiClient).await();

        List<Node> nodes = result.getNodes();
        if (nodes.size() > 0) {
          mNode = nodes.get(0);
        }
      }
    }).start();
  }

  @Override
  public void onConnectionSuspended(int i) {
  }
};

private void sendToPhone(final int value) {
  new Thread(new Runnable() {
    @Override
```

```
      public void run() {
        if( mNode != null ){
          byte[] bytes = ByteBuffer.allocate(4).putInt(value).array();

          Wearable.MessageApi.sendMessage(mGoogleApiClient, mNode.getId(),
            "/dicegame", bytes).await();
        }
      }
    }).start();
  }
}
```

This is just one way of sending an integer. You can also send strings and then parse those to integers on the other end of the pipe. I prefer working with bytes rather than strings. Open MyWearActivity .java and add the code shown in Listing 10-10.

LISTING 10-10: Keeping the screen on

```
package com.wiley.wrox.dicegame;

import android.app.Activity;
import android.hardware.SensorManager;
import android.os.Bundle;
import android.os.CountDownTimer;
import android.support.wearable.view.CircledImageView;
import android.support.wearable.view.WatchViewStub;
import android.view.Window;
import android.view.WindowManager;

import com.google.android.gms.common.ConnectionResult;
import com.google.android.gms.common.api.GoogleApiClient;
import com.google.android.gms.wearable.Node;
import com.google.android.gms.wearable.NodeApi;
import com.google.android.gms.wearable.Wearable;
import com.squareup.seismic.ShakeDetector;

import java.nio.ByteBuffer;
import java.util.List;
import java.util.Random;

public class MyWearActivity extends Activity implements ShakeDetector.Listener {

  private static final int MAX_SHAKE_TIME = 1000;
  private static final int COUNTDOWN_INTERVAL = 100;
  private CircledImageView mCircledImageView;

  private CountDownTimer mCountDownTimer;

  private SensorManager mSensorManager;
  private ShakeDetector mShakeDetector;
```

continues

LISTING 10-10 *(continued)*

```
    private Random mRandom = new Random();

    private GoogleApiClient mGoogleApiClient;
    private Node mNode;

    @Override
    protected void onCreate(Bundle savedInstanceState) {
        super.onCreate(savedInstanceState);
        setContentView(R.layout.activity_my);

        getWindow().addFlags(WindowManager.LayoutParams.FLAG_KEEP_SCREEN_ON);

        ...
    }
    ...
}
```

You may have noticed that on Wear—the sender—we also created a node. The node is the recipient when values are sent. Because we're only sending values from Wear to mobile, and not the other way around, only the Wear needs to have a node.

Keeping the Screen On

The final tweak we'll make is keeping the screen online even if Google doesn't suggest it. With games, you may be inactive while it's your friends' turn to roll their virtual dice. Listing 10-10 shows how to lock the screen.

THE DICE GAME

The finished game includes one six-sided virtual die and a game board. Figure 10-2 shows the user interface of the Wear app as a shake is in progress.

Figure 10-3 shows the game board. It contains only a title and a number—the value of the die.

IMPROVEMENTS

The finished application you've built in this chapter is a simple dice-rolling mechanism. It has no other game mechanics built in, so it's up to you to take it to the next level. Here are some things you can do to improve the game:

➤   Create more intriguing game rules and logic.

➤   Use the number of shakes made as a seed when generating the die value. Doing so can give you another level of control over the game and have players use tactics when shaking their die.

➤   Use more than one sensor for more interesting shake gesture patterns. This could include hidden gestures that are difficult to reproduce but generate higher values.

FIGURE 10-2: The finished Wear app

FIGURE 10-3: The finished mobile app

➤ Improve the user interface by making it more interesting to look at.

➤ Most dice can't get a value of 0, so unless you're making a representation of a very specific die you should make sure to limit the possible values of the die.

SUMMARY

In this chapter you began your journey into the exciting world of gestural interactions. You also had another go at the Google Services APIs for sending data between your mobile and your Wear device.

In the last chapter of this book you'll dive into another exciting realm within wearable programming—smart glasses. You'll get examples of how they work, what features they often have, and how to create your own apps that run on them.

RECOMMENDED READING

Sensors Overview, `http://developer.android.com/guide/topics/sensors/sensors_overview.html`.

Motion Sensor overview, `http://developer.android.com/guide/topics/sensors/sensors_motion.html`.

11

Build Your Own Glass

WHAT'S IN THIS CHAPTER?

➤ The difference between augmented and virtual reality

➤ Review of different wearable glasses

➤ Build your own version of project Cardboard's glasses

➤ Make your smartwatch talk to your DIY glasses

WROX.COM CODE DOWNLOADS FOR THIS CHAPTER

The code downloads for this chapter are found at www.wrox.com/go/androidwearables on the Download Code tab. The code is in the Chapter 11 download and the files are individually named according to filenames noted throughout the chapter.

The first two chapters put wearable computing in context. Wearable gadgets can be placed in three main categories: watches, glasses, and fitness bands.

This book has guided you through the new Wear API from Google, which falls into the first gadget category. Many different vendors sell fitness bands. Chapter 9 discusses making your watch into a pedometer. A whole API called Google Fit is dedicated to the interaction between fitness-related gadgets and handhelds. Many new devices in that category will reach the market in the coming years. Finally, Google Glass has been around since 2012. It is an expensive and hard-to-get gadget. I have been unable to obtain one because I live in Sweden.

Therefore, we approached a vendor—Vuzix—that has a different approach than Google to wearable glasses. Vuzix designs and manufactures glasses with different capabilities. Its design is basically a fully functional mobile phone without 3G connectivity. It is intended for developers and companies interested in creating wearable computer vision applications.

I reviewed Vuzix's M100 Smart Glasses. This interesting product can be mounted on top of any pair of glasses, and is intended for either the left or right eye. It runs one of the latest versions of the Android OS. However, the SDK for this device is not free. Therefore, if on top of having to purchase the device, you need to buy the development environment, it doesn't feel like a good choice for just experimenting and gaining an understanding of the technology's possibilities. Nevertheless, we recommend that you consider this product if you are looking for a standalone device (it works without a handheld) to design a product to, for example, augment a certain process in a production chain.

> **NOTE** *For more information on Vuzix and its products, visit* `http://vuzix.com.`

Not many vendors of wearable devices offer glasses, which makes it kind of hard to pursue what I would love you to experiment with in this chapter. Luckily, two Google engineers realized that the state-of-the-art device for immersive experiences, the Oculus Rift, has screen-related features that are similar to those on a high-end mobile phone. They designed the Google Cardboard project, which this chapter discusses later.

AUGMENTED REALITY AND VIRTUAL REALITY

Let's quickly review the basic concepts related to glasses as interactive devices—specifically, augmented reality (AR) and virtual reality (VR)—before we jump into programming your own application for Cardboard. For just a few bucks, you will be able to build your own VR glasses and connect them to your smartwatch.

Then you will learn how to adjust an existing application to interact with the Wear API. We will take the basic example from the Google Cardboard project and tweak it to communicate with the smartwatch as an input method.

Augmented Reality

Augmented reality implies the addition of computer-generated layers of information to a real image. This means that a user in front of an AR application should see the real world in front of his eyes with an overlay generated by a different source.

AR can be achieved in two ways: through a transparent screen on top of the user's eyes, or through a head-mounted display including cameras that film the environment in real time.

For an AR system to function, it needs to know something about the environment. It needs to know its location, in which direction the user is looking, whether the user is moving, and so on. This kind of information can be obtained through sensors or image analysis.

Common AR experiments use markers to determine either the user's location or the physical location where the system should embed the virtual image on top of the camera feed or real image. In the past I have experimented with a library called NyARToolKit in Java to detect those markers and to add computer-generated shapes to the video feed captured by a webcam into a computer.

Figure 11-1 shows an AR application made with Processing by Amnon Owed. A series of cubes are rendered overlaid on a live video feed captured by a camera. The cubes are rendered on top of a series of markers that have been printed on paper. When the camera captures the image, a library dedicated to AR operations detects the different markers and exposes the geographic coordinates for the programmer to use. In that way it is possible to add any kind of 3D-generated graphics on location on the image as if the 3D objects were in the real physical space.

FIGURE 11-1: Augmented reality application (image courtesy of Amnon Owed)

> **NOTE** *Read the full tutorial on how to generate AR applications in Processing (which in essence is nothing but a Java IDE) at:*
>
> `http://www.creativeapplications.net/processing/augmented-reality-with-processing-tutorial-processing/`
>
> *If you want to know more about Amnon Owed's work, visit* `http://amnonp5.wordpress.com`.

Google Glass has a transparent LCD that generates an overlay of information on top of whatever the user sees. In that sense it is an AR device. The following section has more details.

Google Glass

Google Glass's strength is that it provides the user with an overlay of information on top of whatever he or she perceives thanks to a transparent LCD. Google Glass has some technology on board: it has a camera, some sensors, and the capability to communicate with a handheld. Ever since it was launched at Google I/O in June 2012, it has been the toy everyone in the tech industry wants to play with.

Regardless of its appeal, Google Glass is not a very innovative product. As mentioned in Chapter 1, although researchers have been working on this concept since the 1980s, this is the first time a company has tried to push a concept like this to the mainstream. Its designers intended Google Glass to be a day-to-day device that can be used by anyone in a nonintrusive way.

Figure 11-2 shows Google Glass version 2, a device not yet available.

Project Glass has generated some controversy. Its ubiquitous camera has heated up the discussion about the use of cameras in public spaces. Wearable-computing researcher Steve Mann encountered this issue when he traveled the world wearing his EyeTap device 24/7.

When designing wearable devices for everyday life, you must take into account the difference between what is socially acceptable today and what will be considered acceptable in the near future. Issues such as data ownership and privacy are relevant. Keep that in mind when you create your concepts for new apps.

FIGURE 11-2: Google Glass (image by Mickepanhu, Creative Commons Attribution-ShareAlike 3.0 Unported)

Virtual Reality

VR is quite different from AR. The content in VR can be entirely synthetic. VR starts with the idea of having a head-mounted display that completely covers the user's field of vision. It uses either a display or some sort of projective technology to show information to the user. One example of a VR device is Oculus Rift.

One of the main characteristics of VR is that the head-mounted display must be divided into two sections or one display for each eye. The latest implementations of this type of device use a single high-resolution display and a series of lenses to optically split the image in two. This is how the Oculus Rift operates.

Figure 11-3 shows the back view of the Oculus Rift development kit, dated 2012/2013. The device's characteristic shape has to do with the display at the bottom.

The screen size of the original Oculus Rift display was barely 1280×800 pixels. This is not that much in comparison to the resolution of a high-end handheld. This fact is what inspired Google engineers David Coz and Damien Henry to make

FIGURE 11-3: Oculus Rift (image courtesy of Sebastian Stabinger, CC BY 3.0)

Cardboard—their own VR head-mounted display using just a mobile phone, some cardboard, a couple of lenses, and some other small parts.

VR on a Phone

It is a well-known fact that Google employees have the opportunity to devote 20 percent of their time to other endeavors. That is what Coz and Henry did when they came up with the idea of using a phone and a piece of software to create a VR device.

Contemporary phones have the computing power to run real-time OpenGL environments. Rendering stereoscopic images makes it possible to create a pair of images to stimulate each eye separately, creating the illusion of a real 3D image. You could use as input the images captured by two cameras or simply generate 3D shapes within a virtual world.

The creators of Google Cardboard had the simple but brilliant idea of creating a container for the glasses from inexpensive materials—cardboard in this case. Since the handheld is contained in a box, it is impossible or difficult to interact with the screen. Therefore, the creators considered two alternative input methods: near field communication (NFC) and magnetic fields.

The Cardboard prototype includes an NFC tag that triggers the event of launching a certain app in your phone. A strong neodymium magnet affects the magnetometer in the phone so that it can be used as a button by measuring abrupt changes in the magnetic field.

Figure 11-4 shows the original Google Cardboard, unfolded. The metallic disc is the magnet. The kit includes a pair of lenses and some Velcro as a fastener.

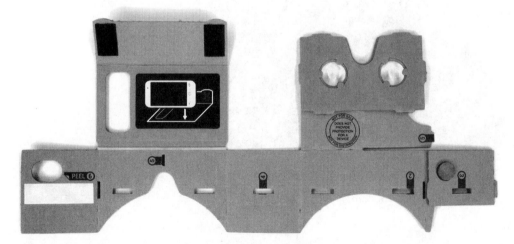

FIGURE 11-4: Unfolded Cardboard (image courtesy of Runner1928 Creative Commons Attribution-ShareAlike 4.0 International)

Currently you can purchase a DIY Google Cardboard kit at several places on the Internet. However, I will guide you through the process of making your own and controlling it from your Wear device instead of using the methods I mentioned: magnet plus NFC.

> **NOTE** *Visit the official Google Cardboard project at* `https://cardboard`
> `.withgoogle.com/.`

BUILDING YOUR OWN GLASSES

If you checked the link I just provided, you saw that part of the fun of the Cardboard project is to make it yourself. Since the arrival of this project in the summer of 2014, several vendors have begun selling their own version of the kit. Prices range between $5 and $30.

To build your own, you just need some cardboard, two small and identical magnifying lenses, some tape, and a rubber band or two. You also need your mobile phone. Don't worry. It won't be harmed during this experiment.

Figure 11-5 shows me wearing my personal Cardboard glasses. I didn't really follow the original design from Google. It takes too many cuts, and I couldn't find the specific type of lenses described on Google's website.

FIGURE 11-5: My personal Cardboard

Lenses

Cheap lenses are usually defined by their focal distance or zoom. The zoom is a multiplier that comes from making a division between the smallest and largest focal distance for a certain magnifying glass. The original Cardboard design recommends using a focal distance of 40mm (1.5 inches).

You can find lenses for as little as $1 up to as much as you want to pay. Cheap lenses are commonly defined by their zoom factor. I found a set of lenses with a 3X zoom for about $6 each at a local hardware store (see Figure 11-6). In my case they seem to be optimal at a distance of 100mm (4 inches) from the phone's screen.

FIGURE 11-6: Lenses

To make your glasses work properly, you will have to fiddle a bit with the design I provide. If the focal distance is not set right, you will see a double image, a blurry one, or some other effect that will not make your experience the best one. Be ready to redo your box a couple of times; I did.

> **NOTE** *You could visit Cardboard's official website to get the original design files for the glasses—they are open source. Producing that design is far more complex as it is intended to be used with a lasercutter. The design suggested here is the Guerrilla version of Cardboard.*

The Simplest Box Possible

This section is about making a box with tape, cardboard, and some love. I started with a cardboard box that was 140 × 200 × 280mm (5.5 × 8 × 11 inches). I broke it open and got a knife and some tape. You can see the design in Figure 11-7. It should not take much effort to copy this design.

The trickiest part is attaching the lenses to the box. With the type of lenses I found, I had to add more tape to the design to make sure they wouldn't move.

Figure 11-8 shows the final design. I kept the lens protectors because they made it easier to attach the lenses to the cardboard box.

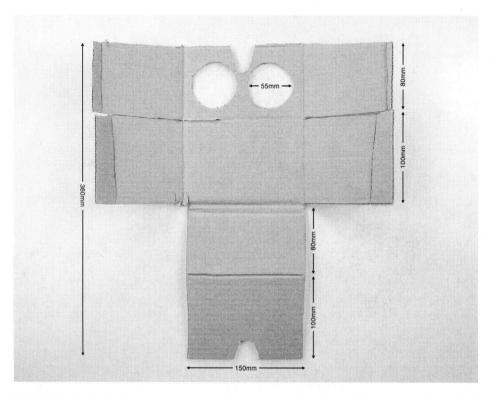

FIGURE 11-7: Box design

FIGURE 11-8: The final version of my Cardboard

THE SIMPLEST APP

The Cardboard documentation page offers a link to a github project that can be used to compile a simple application called "treasure hunt" that allows you to explore all the features of the VR library.

The sample code found today is ready for Android Studio. I have made sure the application compiles as an Android Studio workspace and made it available as a download. I created it starting from an empty Android Wear project for handheld and smartwatch, as explained in earlier chapters.

Figure 11-9 shows what you can expect to see on your screen after you have compiled the application and uploaded it to your handheld. This treasure hunt application was compiled using the Android Studio project provided as a download to this chapter. You can see a cube floating on top of a flat surface using stereoscopic projections. This is the "treasure." You "hunt" for it by pressing the magnet on your Cardboard.

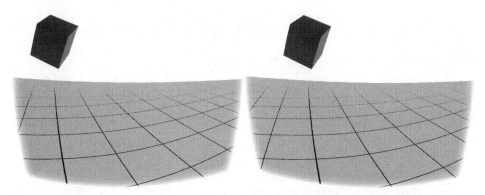

FIGURE 11-9: Treasure hunt app (the colors have been inverted for better visibility)

The goal is to add code to this app so that it uses the Wear API as an input.

> **NOTE** *The simplest sample app for Cardboard can be found at the Cardboard development tutorials at* `https://developers.google.com/cardboard/overview`.
>
> *If you want to see the github project where the original app for this project is located, visit* `https://github.com/googlesamples/cardboard/`.

The cardboard.jar Library

The key to making the stereoscopic projection work is including in your project the VR Toolkit .jar file. This library is responsible for all the complex operations regarding the stereoscopic imaging and also adds access to the sensors.

You can find the binary version of the library at the github project mentioned in the preceding section. You should remember to add it to your compilation path. I recommend that you start working with the code example I created, which includes this binary already.

The following sections show you briefly how things work. It is not the goal of this chapter to teach you specifically about Google Cardboard, but about integrating an existing app with Android Wear.

Looking at the Code

We will start by looking at the main activity in the program. The idea is to understand how it works in order to find places to patch it. The example uses the magnetometer as a button. I will later substitute that functionality to use the smartwatch instead.

The Glasses' MyActivityPhone.java

This class configures the use of the VR Toolkit library, as shown in Listing 11-1.

LISTING 11-1: Main Activity's onCreate method (filename: `MyActivityPhone.java`)

```
package com.wiley.wrox.chapter11.cardboardglass;

import android.os.Bundle;
import android.content.Context;
import android.opengl.GLES20;
import android.opengl.Matrix;
import android.os.Vibrator;
import android.util.Log;
import com.google.vrtoolkit.cardboard.*;

import javax.microedition.khronos.egl.EGLConfig;
import java.io.BufferedReader;
import java.io.IOException;
import java.io.InputStream;
import java.io.InputStreamReader;
import java.nio.ByteBuffer;
import java.nio.ByteOrder;
import java.nio.FloatBuffer;

public class MyActivityPhone extends CardboardActivity
    implements CardboardView.StereoRenderer {
[...]
    /**
     * Sets the view to our CardboardView and initializes the
     * transformation matrices we will use to render our scene.
     * @param savedInstanceState
     */
    @Override
    protected void onCreate(Bundle savedInstanceState) {
        super.onCreate(savedInstanceState);
        setContentView(R.layout.activity_my_phone);

        CardboardView cardboardView =
            (CardboardView) findViewById(R.id.cardboard_view);
        cardboardView.setRenderer(this);
```

```
        setCardboardView(cardboardView);

        mModelCube = new float[16];
        mCamera = new float[16];
        mView = new float[16];
        mModelViewProjection = new float[16];
        mModelView = new float[16];
        mModelFloor = new float[16];
        mHeadView = new float[16];
        mVibrator = (Vibrator) getSystemService(Context.VIBRATOR_SERVICE);


        mOverlayView = (CardboardOverlayView) findViewById(R.id.overlay);
        mOverlayView.show3DToast("Pull the magnet when you find an object.");
    }
[...]
```

I have highlighted a few things in this code:

➤ Notice that the VR Toolkit from Google is needed for the code to compile.

➤ In the overridden version of onCreate(), after setting up the view and the renderer and initializing all the variables, the program initializes an instance of the vibrator. It gives the user physical feedback.

➤ When the program starts, it projects a sentence in the 3D space: "Pull the magnet when you find an object." This gives a hint of what the user is expected to do when interacting with this application. This is one of the main aspects of our intervention in this code. We will get rid of the magnet and use the watch instead.

Listing 11-2 focuses on the onCardboardTrigger()method within the main class. This method is called when the magnet detects a sudden change in the magnetic field. With isLookingAtObject() it checks whether the handheld has rotated to an angle so that the user is facing a floating cube—the treasure in this game. If that is the case, a success message appears onscreen. If not, the user is encouraged to keep searching. Regardless of whether the user finds the object, the phone vibrates.

LISTING 11-2: onCardboardTrigger method (filename: MyActivityPhone.java)

```
/**
 * Increment the score, hide the object, and give feedback if the
 * user pulls the magnet while looking at the object. Otherwise,
 * remind the user what to do.
 */
@Override
public void onCardboardTrigger() {
    Log.i(TAG, "onCardboardTrigger");

    if (isLookingAtObject()) {
        mScore++;
        mOverlayView.show3DToast("Found it! Look around for" +
            "another one.\nScore = " + mScore);
        hideObject();
```

continues

LISTING 11-2: *(continued)*

```
    } else {
        mOverlayView.show3DToast("Look around to find the object!");
    }
    // Always give user feedback
    mVibrator.vibrate(50);
}
```

Listing 11-3 shows the isLookingAtObject() method, which happens to be part of the code and not part of the library. It uses a series of methods belonging to the VR Toolkit library that aren't within the scope of this experiment. I think it is worth taking a quick look at them just to see that they aren't that scary.

LISTING 11-3: isLookingAtObject method (filename: MyActivityPhone.java)

```java
/**
 * Check if user is looking at object by calculating where
 * the object is in eye-space.
 * @return
 */
private boolean isLookingAtObject() {
    float[] initVec = {0, 0, 0, 1.0f};
    float[] objPositionVec = new float[4];

    // Convert object space to camera space. Use the headView from onNewFrame.
    Matrix.multiplyMM(mModelView, 0, mHeadView, 0, mModelCube, 0);
    Matrix.multiplyMV(objPositionVec, 0, mModelView, 0, initVec, 0);

    float pitch = (float)Math.atan2(objPositionVec[1], -objPositionVec[2]);
    float yaw = (float)Math.atan2(objPositionVec[0], -objPositionVec[2]);

    Log.i(TAG, "Object position: X: " + objPositionVec[0]
            + "  Y: " + objPositionVec[1] + " Z: " + objPositionVec[2]);
    Log.i(TAG, "Object Pitch: " + pitch +"  Yaw: " + yaw);

    return (Math.abs(pitch) < PITCH_LIMIT) && (Math.abs(yaw) < YAW_LIMIT);
}
```

In essence, the code checks whether the camera angle in the 3D environment the user is navigating is within the limits that should allow the user to see it floating over the ground. I highlighted the last line in the method, showing the logical statement that determines whether the conditions indicate that the user is looking at a cube.

The Glasses' AndroidManifest.xml

Listing 11-4 shows the manifest file for the glasses. It highlights two different parts:

➤ A uses-permission tag to allow the app to use the NFC tag reader

➤ A uses-permission tag to allow the app to use the haptic feedback through the handheld's vibrator

LISTING 11-4: Glasses' manifest file (filename: `AndroidManifest.xml`)

```xml
<?xml version="1.0" encoding="utf-8"?>
<manifest xmlns:android="http://schemas.android.com/apk/res/android"
    package="com.wiley.wrox.chapter11.cardboardglass" >

    <uses-permission android:name="android.permission.NFC" />
    <uses-permission android:name="android.permission.VIBRATE" />
    <uses-feature android:glEsVersion="0x00020000" android:required="true" />

    <application
        android:allowBackup="true"
        android:icon="@drawable/ic_launcher"
        android:label="@string/app_name"
        android:theme="@style/AppTheme" >
        <activity
            android:screenOrientation="landscape"
            android:name=".MyActivityPhone"
            android:label="@string/app_name" >
            <intent-filter>
                <action android:name="android.intent.action.MAIN" />

                <category android:name="android.intent.category.LAUNCHER" />
            </intent-filter>
        </activity>
    </application>

</manifest>
```

A Couple More Classes

Two more Java files are included in the phone's part of the project. One handles the layout of the information on the 3D visualization, and the other contains simple information about the 3D objects. I will show you two code snippets to help you understand the content of those files. You could hack them easily to get them to do things differently.

Listing 11-5 shows an excerpt of `CardboardOverlayView`, a class that extends the linear layout to include two different visualizations: one for the left eye and one for the right.

LISTING 11-5: Excerpt of the CardboardOverlayView class (filename: `CardboardOverlayView.java`)

```java
package com.wiley.wrox.chapter11.cardboardglass;

import [...]

/**
 * Contains two subviews to provide a simple stereo HUD.
 */
public class CardboardOverlayView extends LinearLayout {
    private static final String TAG = CardboardOverlayView.class.getSimpleName();
```

continues

LISTING 11-5: *(continued)*

```
    private final CardboardOverlayEyeView mLeftView;
    private final CardboardOverlayEyeView mRightView;
    private AlphaAnimation mTextFadeAnimation;

    public CardboardOverlayView(Context context, AttributeSet attrs) {
        super(context, attrs);
        setOrientation(HORIZONTAL);

        LayoutParams params = new LayoutParams(
            LayoutParams.MATCH_PARENT, LayoutParams.MATCH_PARENT, 1.0f);
        params.setMargins(0, 0, 0, 0);

        mLeftView = new CardboardOverlayEyeView(context, attrs);
        mLeftView.setLayoutParams(params);
        addView(mLeftView);

        mRightView = new CardboardOverlayEyeView(context, attrs);
        mRightView.setLayoutParams(params);
        addView(mRightView);

        // Set some reasonable defaults.
        setDepthOffset(0.016f);
        setColor(Color.rgb(150, 255, 180));
        setVisibility(View.VISIBLE);

        mTextFadeAnimation = new AlphaAnimation(1.0f, 0.0f);
        mTextFadeAnimation.setDuration(5000);
    }

    public void show3DToast(String message) {
        setText(message);
        setTextAlpha(1f);
        mTextFadeAnimation.setAnimationListener(new EndAnimationListener() {
            @Override
            public void onAnimationEnd(Animation animation) {
                setTextAlpha(0f);
            }
        });
        startAnimation(mTextFadeAnimation);
    }
[...]
```

I have chosen two methods in the class that I consider relevant to understanding how it works. First is the constructor, where you can see objects that display the data for each eye. Second is the show3DToast() method, which shows the text floating in front of your eyes while you navigate the 3D space. The rest of the class is basically a series of methods. They handle listeners as well as how to show text. More importantly, a helper class (not shown here) sets the layout of the canvas and text area for each eye.

Listing 11-6 shows an excerpt of WorldLayoutData, a class containing general information about the objects in the world. In this case, the array under the display contains information about the color of the cubes before the user finds them. "Finding" is the action of acknowledging having found the cube.

```java
public static final float[] CUBE_COLORS = new float[] {
        // front, green
        0f, 0.5273f, 0.2656f, 1.0f,
        0f, 0.5273f, 0.2656f, 1.0f,
        0f, 0.5273f, 0.2656f, 1.0f,
        0f, 0.5273f, 0.2656f, 1.0f,
        0f, 0.5273f, 0.2656f, 1.0f,
        0f, 0.5273f, 0.2656f, 1.0f,

        // right, blue
        0.0f, 0.3398f, 0.9023f, 1.0f,
        0.0f, 0.3398f, 0.9023f, 1.0f,
        0.0f, 0.3398f, 0.9023f, 1.0f,
        0.0f, 0.3398f, 0.9023f, 1.0f,
        0.0f, 0.3398f, 0.9023f, 1.0f,
        0.0f, 0.3398f, 0.9023f, 1.0f,

        // back, also green
        0f, 0.5273f, 0.2656f, 1.0f,
        0f, 0.5273f, 0.2656f, 1.0f,
        0f, 0.5273f, 0.2656f, 1.0f,
        0f, 0.5273f, 0.2656f, 1.0f,
        0f, 0.5273f, 0.2656f, 1.0f,
        0f, 0.5273f, 0.2656f, 1.0f,

        // left, also blue
        0.0f, 0.3398f, 0.9023f, 1.0f,
        0.0f, 0.3398f, 0.9023f, 1.0f,
        0.0f, 0.3398f, 0.9023f, 1.0f,
        0.0f, 0.3398f, 0.9023f, 1.0f,
        0.0f, 0.3398f, 0.9023f, 1.0f,
        0.0f, 0.3398f, 0.9023f, 1.0f,

        // top, red
        0.8359375f,     0.17578125f,     0.125f, 1.0f,
        0.8359375f,     0.17578125f,     0.125f, 1.0f,
        0.8359375f,     0.17578125f,     0.125f, 1.0f,
        0.8359375f,     0.17578125f,     0.125f, 1.0f,
        0.8359375f,     0.17578125f,     0.125f, 1.0f,
        0.8359375f,     0.17578125f,     0.125f, 1.0f,

        // bottom, also red
        0.8359375f,     0.17578125f,     0.125f, 1.0f,
        0.8359375f,     0.17578125f,     0.125f, 1.0f,
        0.8359375f,     0.17578125f,     0.125f, 1.0f,
        0.8359375f,     0.17578125f,     0.125f, 1.0f,
        0.8359375f,     0.17578125f,     0.125f, 1.0f,
        0.8359375f,     0.17578125f,     0.125f, 1.0f,
};
```

Once you execute this application on your Cardboard, the result you can expect will look like Figure 11-9.

Getting Your Cardboard to Talk to Your Smartwatch

Following the code examples from Chapter 7, it should be pretty straightforward to make your watch the input device to the app I just showed you. You import a couple of classes, modify the manifest file, include the Wearable API to send messages back and forth, make your own wearable app, and hack the `onCardboardTrigger()`method in your phone's main activity. Piece of cake!

Let's do this step by step. You will build two apps that will be connected through Google Play services. The watch displays the screen with a black background. When touched, it sends a message to the handheld indicating this. It also toggles the color. This example is unidirectional: We will send data from the wearable app to the phone app, but not the other way around. Implementing the communication in the other direction is not difficult using the code examples from previous chapters.

As in Chapter 7, you must take into account two things when dealing with such a scenario:

➤ How will you handle communication between devices? I will try using the Data API.

➤ How will you update the information on the devices' screens? Like the case explored in Chapter 7, I will follow an event-based approach with a thread that responds to the arrival of data by changing the UI.

Start from the Previous Project

Start from the example we just finished. It contains all the code needed for building the Cardboard. You just need to patch the `MyActivityPhone` class in a couple of places. The project I prepared for you in the download area for this chapter includes a clean class for the Android Wear device.

The first step is to create the API client. You need only one object of the class `DataItem` shared between both devices, where one field represents the event of having touched the watch's screen.

As usual, I will provide code snippets to give you an understanding of the code. For full code listings, check this chapter's downloads.

The Phone's MyActivityPhone.java

In MyActivityPhone.java, shown in Listing 11-7, you have to add a couple of things:

➤ The declaration of a Google API client to start sharing data between devices, with overrides to control the possibility of the connectivity's being lost or not even started

➤ A local broadcast manager to capture the intents sent by the class listening to the data arriving from the smartwatch

LISTING 11-7: Modifications to the main activity on the phone app (filename: `MyActivityPhone.java`)

```
[...]
private GoogleApiClient mGoogleApiClient;

private BroadcastReceiver mResultReceiver;
 [...]
@Override
```

```java
protected void onCreate(Bundle savedInstanceState) {
    super.onCreate(savedInstanceState);
    setContentView(R.layout.activity_my_phone);

    // declaration of the Google API client
    mGoogleApiClient = new GoogleApiClient.Builder(this)
            .addConnectionCallbacks(new GoogleApiClient.ConnectionCallbacks() {
                @Override
                public void onConnected(Bundle connectionHint) {
                    Log.v(TAG, "Connection established");
                }
                @Override
                public void onConnectionSuspended(int cause) {
                    Log.v(TAG, "Connection suspended");
                }
            })
            .addOnConnectionFailedListener(new
                GoogleApiClient.OnConnectionFailedListener() {
                @Override
                public void onConnectionFailed(ConnectionResult result) {
                    Log.v(TAG, "Connection failed");
                }
            })
            .addApi(Wearable.API)
            .build();
    mGoogleApiClient.connect();
    mResultReceiver = createBroadcastReceiver();
    LocalBroadcastManager.getInstance(this).registerReceiver(
        mResultReceiver,
        new IntentFilter("cardboard.localIntent"));

    CardboardView cardboardView = (CardboardView)
        findViewById(R.id.cardboard_view);
    cardboardView.setRenderer(this);
    setCardboardView(cardboardView);

    mModelCube = new float[16];
    mCamera = new float[16];
    mView = new float[16];
    mModelViewProjection = new float[16];
    mModelView = new float[16];
    mModelFloor = new float[16];
    mHeadView = new float[16];
    mVibrator = (Vibrator) getSystemService(Context.VIBRATOR_SERVICE);


    mOverlayView = (CardboardOverlayView) findViewById(R.id.overlay);
    mOverlayView.show3DToast("Pull the magnet when you find an object.");
}
[...]
    private void onWearTouch() {
        Log.v(TAG, "Arrived touch event");

        if (isLookingAtObject()) {
```

LISTING 11-7: *(continued)*

```
                mScore++;
                mOverlayView.show3DToast("Found it! Look around "+
                    "for another one.\nScore = " + mScore);
                hideObject();
            } else {
                mOverlayView.show3DToast("Look around to find the object!");
            }
            // Always give user feedback
            mVibrator.vibrate(50);
        }

        @Override
        protected void onDestroy() {
            if (mResultReceiver != null) {
                LocalBroadcastManager.getInstance(this)
                    .unregisterReceiver(mResultReceiver);
            }
            super.onDestroy();
        }

        private BroadcastReceiver createBroadcastReceiver() {
            // we are just interested in the event, the rest doesn't matter
            return new BroadcastReceiver() {
                @Override
                public void onReceive(Context context, Intent intent) {
                    onWearTouch();
                }
            };
        }
```

As you can see, the basic idea is to call a method from the `BroadcastReceiver` and then perform a series of actions onscreen. In this case, it adds a point to the user's record and vibrates. On top of that, you don't need to sacrifice the possibility of using the magnet as an input. These new methods enhance your app without giving away anything (unless you want to do so).

The Phone's AndroidManifest.xml

The service declaration is highlighted in Listing 11-8. This, together with the metadata tag declaring the use of the Google Play services API, are the two changes needed for the service to boot when the app launches and for the combo to use the Google Play Services API to talk to the other device.

LISTING 11-8: Full manifest file (filename: `AndroidManifest.xml`)

```
<?xml version="1.0" encoding="utf-8"?>
<manifest xmlns:android="http://schemas.android.com/apk/res/android"
    package="com.wiley.wrox.chapter11.cardboardglass" >

    <uses-permission android:name="android.permission.NFC" />
```

```
<uses-permission android:name="android.permission.VIBRATE" />
<uses-feature android:glEsVersion="0x00020000" android:required="true" />

<application
    android:allowBackup="true"
    android:icon="@drawable/ic_launcher"
    android:label="@string/app_name"
    android:theme="@style/AppTheme" >
    <activity
      android:screenOrientation="landscape"
      android:name="MyActivityPhone"
      android:label="@string/app_name" >
        <intent-filter>
            <action android:name="android.intent.action.MAIN" />

            <category android:name="android.intent.category.LAUNCHER" />
        </intent-filter>
    </activity>
    <service android:name=
"DataLayerListenerServicePhone" >
        <intent-filter>
            <action
android:name="com.google.android.gms.wearable.BIND_LISTENER" />
        </intent-filter>
    </service>

    <meta-data android:name="com.google.android.gms.version"
        android:value="@integer/google_play_services_version" />
</application>

</manifest>
```

The Phone's DataLayerListenerService

DataLayerListenerService is launched on the phone after the app launches. When the phone registers an event of any of the shared data objects changing, the listener is triggered. In this case it filters by WEAR2PHONE. This object, as defined in MyActivityWear.java (see the source code in the next section), sends a boolean variable each time the screen is touched. The variable arriving from the Wear device toggles between true and false upon data arrival as a way to show progress.

Listing 11-9 shows the listener waiting for data to arrive from the watch. It is very similar to the one used in the last example of Chapter 7, only that this time there is no data going back from the phone to the watch.

LISTING 11-9: Full listener on the phone (filename: DataLayerListenerService.java)

```java
package com.wiley.wrox.chapter11.cardboardglass;

import android.net.Uri;
import android.util.Log;

import com.google.android.gms.common.data.FreezableUtils;
```

continues

LISTING 11-9: *(continued)*

```
import com.google.android.gms.wearable.DataEvent;
import com.google.android.gms.wearable.DataEventBuffer;
import com.google.android.gms.wearable.DataMap;
import com.google.android.gms.wearable.DataMapItem;
import com.google.android.gms.wearable.WearableListenerService;

import java.util.List;

public class DataLayerListenerServicePhone extends WearableListenerService {

    private static String TAG = "wrox-mobile";
    @Override
    public void onDataChanged(DataEventBuffer dataEvents) {
        super.onDataChanged(dataEvents);

        Log.v(TAG, "Data arrived");

        final List<DataEvent> events =
                FreezableUtils.freezeIterable(dataEvents);
        for(DataEvent event : events) {
            final Uri uri = event.getDataItem().getUri();
            final String path = uri!=null ? uri.getPath() : null;
            if("/WEAR2PHONE".equals(path)) {
                final DataMap map =
                    DataMapItem.fromDataItem(event.getDataItem()).getDataMap();
                // read your values from map:
                boolean touch = map.getBoolean("touch");
                String reply = "Touched:" + touch;
                Log.v(TAG, reply);
                // if there was a touch, trigger the event detection
                Intent localIntent = new Intent("cardboard.localIntent");
                localIntent.putExtra("result", touch);
                LocalBroadcastManager.getInstance(this)
                    .sendBroadcast(localIntent);
            }
        }
    }
}
```

MyActivityWear.java

The activity on the watch (as shown on Listing 11-10) is simple. It needs to initialize the use of the data API and send data whenever the screen is touched. To make this easier to understand and to give the user visual feedback, the following things happen:

➤ The data is sent as WEAR2PHONE.

➤ The background color changes at each press. If the screen was white, it turns black, and vice versa.

➤ touchListener is implemented within the method dedicated to the layout. That's where the action happens.

LISTING 11-10: Main activity class on the wearable (filename: MyActivityWear.java)

```java
package com.wiley.wrox.chapter11.cardboardglass;

import android.app.Activity;
import android.graphics.Color;
import android.os.Bundle;
import android.support.wearable.view.WatchViewStub;
import android.util.Log;
import android.view.MotionEvent;
import android.view.View;
import android.widget.TextView;

import com.google.android.gms.common.ConnectionResult;
import com.google.android.gms.common.api.GoogleApiClient;
import com.google.android.gms.wearable.DataMap;
import com.google.android.gms.wearable.PutDataMapRequest;
import com.google.android.gms.wearable.Wearable;

public class MyActivityWear extends Activity {

    private GoogleApiClient mGoogleApiClient;

    private TextView mTextView;
    private int mColor = Color.rgb(255,255,255);
    private boolean mTouch = false;
    private static final  String TAG = "wrox-wear";

    @Override
    protected void onCreate(Bundle savedInstanceState) {
        super.onCreate(savedInstanceState);
        setContentView(R.layout.activity_my_wear);

        mGoogleApiClient = new GoogleApiClient.Builder(this)
                .addConnectionCallbacks(new
                    GoogleApiClient.ConnectionCallbacks() {
                    @Override
                    public void onConnected(Bundle connectionHint) {
                        Log.v(TAG, "Connection established");
                    }
                    @Override
                    public void onConnectionSuspended(int cause) {
                        Log.v(TAG, "Connection suspended");
                    }
                })
                .addOnConnectionFailedListener(new
                    GoogleApiClient.OnConnectionFailedListener() {
                    @Override
                    public void onConnectionFailed(ConnectionResult result) {
                        Log.v(TAG, "Connection failed");
```

continues

LISTING 11-10: *(continued)*

```java
                        }
                    })
                    .addApi(Wearable.API)
                    .build();
            mGoogleApiClient.connect();

            final WatchViewStub stub = (WatchViewStub)
                findViewById(R.id.watch_view_stub);
            stub.setOnLayoutInflatedListener(new
            WatchViewStub.OnLayoutInflatedListener() {
             @Override
             public void onLayoutInflated(WatchViewStub stub) {
                mTextView = (TextView) stub.findViewById(R.id.text);

                stub.setOnTouchListener(new View.OnTouchListener() {
                    @Override
                    public boolean onTouch(View view, MotionEvent event) {
                        Log.v(TAG, "UI touched");
                        toggleBackgroundColor();

                        if(mGoogleApiClient==null)
                            return false;

                        final PutDataMapRequest putRequest =
                            PutDataMapRequest.create("/WEAR2PHONE");
                        final DataMap map = putRequest.getDataMap();
                        mTouch = !mTouch;
                        map.putBoolean("touch", mTouch);
                        Wearable.DataApi.putDataItem(mGoogleApiClient,
                            putRequest.asPutDataRequest());

                        return false;
                    }
                });
             }
            });
        }

        private void toggleBackgroundColor(){
            if (mColor == Color.rgb(0, 0, 0))
                mColor = Color.rgb(255, 255, 255);
            else
                mColor = Color.rgb(0, 0, 0);
            setBackgroundColor(mColor);
        }

        private void setBackgroundColor(int color) {
            final WatchViewStub stub = (WatchViewStub)
                findViewById(R.id.watch_view_stub);
            stub.setBackgroundColor(color);
        }
    }
```

The Wear Android Manifest File

The only difference between the manifest file shown in Listing 11-11 and the default one when you create a new project is the call to Google Play that lets the wearable talk to the handheld inside your Cardboard glasses.

LISTING 11-11: Manifest file on the wearable (filename: `AndroidManifest.xml`**)**

```xml
<?xml version="1.0" encoding="utf-8"?>
<manifest xmlns:android="http://schemas.android.com/apk/res/android"
    package="com.wiley.wrox.chapter11.cardboardglass" >

    <uses-feature android:name="android.hardware.type.watch" />

    <application
        android:allowBackup="true"
        android:icon="@drawable/ic_launcher"
        android:label="@string/app_name"
        android:theme="@android:style/Theme.DeviceDefault" >
        <activity
android:name=
"MyActivityWear"
            android:label="@string/app_name" >
            <intent-filter>
                <action android:name="android.intent.action.MAIN" />

                <category android:name="android.intent.category.LAUNCHER" />
            </intent-filter>
        </activity>

        <meta-data android:name="com.google.android.gms.version"
            android:value="@integer/google_play_services_version" />
    </application>

</manifest>
```

The Final Result

As usual, I recommend that you check the full example in the file `chapter11_CardboardGlass_touch.zip`. There you will find all the code used for this example, ready for you to copy and start experimenting with in your own applications.

The expected result on your side should look like Figure 11-9, which shows the activity on my phone. When touching the screen of your wearable and being in front of a cube (it will be highlighted in yellow), you earn a point.

SUMMARY

You have learned how to integrate Wear into an existing block of code. In this chapter we enhanced the functionality of an existing app by adding touch interaction through the wearable.

You also had a chance to experiment with one of the most promising libraries of code in the world of DIY head-mounted displays—the VR Toolkit used to power Google Cardboard.

From a more theoretical standpoint, you were introduced to augmented reality and virtual reality. You read about the different products you can use to build experiences for both.

INDEX